£1-50

A MOTHER'S
GUIDE
TO LIFE

Also by Barbara Toner

A MOTHER'S GUIDE TO LIFE

Barbara Toner

Hodder & Stoughton

First published in 1997 by Hodder and Stoughton
A division of Hodder Headline PLC

British Library Cataloguing in Publication Data

Toner, Barbara
A mother's guide to life
1. Mothers – Life skills guides
I. Title
306.8'743

ISBN 0 340 68977 3

Typeset by Palimpsest Book Production Limited,
Polmont, Stirlingshire
Printed and bound in Great Britain by
Mackays of Chatham PLC, Chatham, Kent

Hodder and Stoughton
A division of Hodder Headline PLC
338 Euston Road
London NW1 3BH

To Helen, best mother in the world

CONTENTS

An introduction

Dear Daughters,

Maybe I have misled you into thinking you know everything already. You are, as I've told you many times, the cleverest, wittiest, most musical and ravishing girls who ever lived and what's more, we have spent a fortune on your education. The other day, however, after too much coffee which made me hyperventilate, I got to worrying about death and I thought, 'They know nothing. I have told them nothing.' I'm writing you this guide because I would be failing you as a mother if I didn't.

There are many peculiar, difficult and distressing people and circumstances for which you should be prepared. If I had my way I'd split myself into three and follow you around day and night to punch people who offended you, to butt in with advice at every crossroad and to clutch you to my heart at every pain. But I can't and your father would have me committed if I could, so I am giving you this book to learn by heart.

You may say, 'But Mumma, you haven't stopped talking since we were born,' and to that I reply, 'But how much have you heard?' You may also say, 'We will learn the hard way just as you did.' My response to that is, 'Why go my hard way when I now see the way round it?'

There are many things I don't know for sure, you may be surprised to hear – I'm not one hundred per cent up on the money market – but what I can tell you with conviction is what happened to me, what I did about it and the lessons therein. Some of it you will have witnessed for yourself but won't have appreciated. It's not until you're quite old that you can tell for certain your mother has blundered badly, wonder why and forgive her.

Owing to an impetuous nature and sorry tendency to speak out of turn, my life has been full of blunders. Uncannily, it has also been a fortunate one. I wanted to be a writer from the time I could read and I have become one. I have been married for a very long time to a man who has always been gracious enough to accept me the way I am. We had you and you have never been less than a constant source of joy, pleasure and heart-stopping pride.

By dint of astonishing time management, I have been able to have a full-time career and be a full-time mother. My greatest skill, as you know, is time management and I will be telling you about beta-blockers, how to pretend to be in two places at the same time without a mobile phone and the recipe for a three-minute sponge.

It may be that your own lives will be very different. The paths women tread are now so many and varied. God knows I have tried to read your futures through imaging and psychic powers, but the truth is, no matter how hard I've willed it and how hard I've clutched your jewellery in my hand, I've never seen anything apart from those little dots you get when the sun shines through your lashes. Maybe if I'd been able to get my wedding ring off, the channels would have been clearer.

Your lives will be what the heavens decree and what you make of them. I hope with all my heart they will be happy and fulfilling but no matter how satisfactory any life is in its broad sweep, there will always be moments of anguish, always causes for panic, concern, rage and bewilderment. Many of them will be in a kitchen with a man in it.

My intention is to spare you what I can with the benefit of my hindsight. I don't know how much use it will be to you, but passing it on will make me feel a whole lot better about drinking too much coffee.

*Your ever loving,
Mumma.*

INSPIRATIONAL STUFF

THE MEANING OF LIFE AND HOW IT SHOULD BE LIVED

What is the point, you will wonder from time to time. My advice is not to trouble yourself. Contemplate, by all means, the notion of infinite time, space, what Adam and Eve looked like and universal consciousness, but don't get bogged down in it. It will only make you ill. More helpful is to ask, not why am I here, but what do I do now I am.

This will lead to daydreaming and list-making, both of which will sharpen your sense of purpose. You need a sense of purpose. It is the correct means to most ends. The end you are seeking is a happy and productive life and if you don't have one it will be your own fault. God willing.

YOUR OWN TWO FEET

Some lives are sorely afflicted by acts of God, so-called because they happen, there's nothing you can do about it and you have to blame someone. They include famine,

plague and pestilence. Should you find yourself in
a plague situation, bear up (see The Right Attitude).
More than likely, your lives will only be assailed by
the regular challenges of survival and aspiration in a
western democracy. These should be met with vigour.
They will probably include a career, a marriage, council
tax and asthma, but you will manage.

You have been born with an intellect, a will and
the power to choose, so you can and must accept
responsibility for yourself. This doesn't happen
overnight but by the time you are thirty or so. Call it
forty. For many years prior to this you will be struggling
to stand on your own two feet but I will be clingy as I
am unnaturally overprotective and possibly a little bit
controlling.

BE GRATEFUL

Even so, I want you to know that life is a privilege and
to waste it is sinful. You didn't ask to be born but you
were, against all odds, therefore you should be grateful.
When you think I stuck a burning cigarette into your
father's ear on our second night out, you'll understand
what a near thing it was.

In view of the privilege, you must use what talents
you have to the best of your ability and contribute
somehow to the common good. Your conscience will
connect you to the common good and if you want to
sleep at night, you should listen to it. I know you will
because we come from a long line of fretters.

THE COMMON GOOD

This doesn't mean you have to be a missionary. I don't want to be a missionary even though I promised myself to God when I was eleven and have a dreadful feeling I will be called after the menopause although I have a horror of life in a mud hut. No. You just have to chip in where needed. Forget the time I sent you to work in an old folks' home so you would appreciate your fortunate lot. I see now how miserable that was for the old folks.

The common good will present itself to you every day: a friend will want to talk endlessly about herself; an old lady will need help crossing the road and talk endlessly about herself (possibly me); your father will want his stapler back. This is goodness at its most basic but you will improve if you practise. Self-sacrifice is the key to being a better person. Don't go overboard. Martyrs are social failures.

THE BEST OF YOUR ABILITY

Where will the best of your ability get you, you want to know. Will you triumph on the world stage and have glittering prizes heaped upon you as leaders in your field? I'm only guessing. But yes.

You have inherited your father's multiple talents and my energy. You are smart, employable, motivated and know how to use your contacts. You only have to work hard, get the breaks, read the wind, speak your mind and so forth. But is that what you want? It's a mistake to imagine your job is what you are or that your success as a human being depends on great career moves. We didn't educate you for nothing. But learn to value yourself for what you are because the value of others is never reliable.

WHAT ARE YOU

Some people live their whole lives and never think they are anything. They die never knowing what they were and it's not an easy death. They imagine they have failed because they never got to be what they thought their talents merited. Or they never got to be anything because they thought they had no talent. Or they never got to be anything because they never knew what they wanted to be. You could slap these people as they expire. Everyone is something. The very best thing you can be is contented.

With this in mind, you must allow a little flexibility into your sense of purpose. There are, as your grandfather used to say, a hundred ways to skin a rabbit. Who's to say you can't start life as a no-hoper and end up with a Pulitzer prize? Plenty of people have. Who's to say you might not forsake everything for a mud hut? Provided you are happy, though don't imagine for a minute that I will be should this be your choice.

An acceptance of what you are and where you fit into the grand scheme of things is all you need, whether you end up rich, poor, fat or thin, at the top of the tree or dangling off a bottom branch. I urge you to accept the idea of a grand scheme because it helps you to accept some things are just not meant to be without understanding exactly why at the time.

Failure isn't not succeeding; it's not trying your hardest and not contributing, however modestly or rarely, to the common good.

GOD IN MY EXPERIENCE

You may find a sense of purpose in religion. You have been baptised but may just as easily decide you are a follower of the Great Wandjini. You might prefer mucking around with crystals. Whatever brings you comfort.

I found myself at odds with the nuns early in my life. When I expressed the view that I hadn't been given the gift of faith at baptism they said, 'Leave the room.' Since then I have been an atheist, an agnostic and now it comforts me to believe there is a universal consciousness. I've no idea what it means; it's just my something greater than all of us which receives prayer. As you know, I am keen on prayer and I recommend it to you as a way of exerting influence when all other avenues are looking dodgy.

I pray for your safety, I pray for people in car accidents and I pray for happy outcomes. I get your grandmother to pray as well. She is excellent at it and has very good results. She says she isn't holy because she is too uncharitable but I think she is. She certainly looks holy and she did a great job with the lump in our friend's nipple.

I don't know what will bring you spiritual peace but I know you should seek it. Whatever it is won't work for you unless it provides a system of values with which you are at ease. This system won't be the point of life, but sticking to it gives you something to live by and up to.

Somewhere in there should be don't lie, don't steal, love your neighbour and to thine own self be true. Also, honour thy father and thy mother which I know you will eventually. There are obvious exceptions to all the above but they provide a very good rule of thumb and

I believe they are in harmony with the grand scheme of things. Whatever it is.

THE GREAT BEYOND

Twenty-five years ago, someone accused me of having no sense of mysticism and I have never forgiven him. I don't know if mysticism is part of the meaning of life but the great prophets have all been mystics and frankly, I don't think it's visible to the naked eye and how dare anyone tell me I'm not something.

It's my belief that everyone is mystic to a greater or lesser extent and some people think they have visions. I am not one although there's no ignoring my psychic flashes. And there's no denying the tarot is spookily accurate or that astrologers get a lot of stuff right. I think this means that we have a long way to go up the evolutionary hill.

I would counsel you not to put too much store by mysticism or you will soon go off your rocker and lose your grip on reality. The man who accused me of having none finished up on the bottle.

A FACT OF LIFE

The most brutal fact of life is that it ends and even though we may die surrounded by our nearest and dearest, wherever we go next, we go on our own. Knowing this, the best advice I can offer is that you live in the present. You can learn from the past and plan for the future but live in the present. This means getting pleasure from the moment and giving the moment your all. I don't think it will make you a better person. But it will make you happier and your lives richer, then when you die, you will have nothing to complain about.

Rule: Don't bother with the spiritual healing centre at the bottom of our road. I went there once for stress relief and the masseuse didn't turn up.

THE RIGHT ATTITUDE

You all have looks, intelligence, a good ear for music and ball skills and these are blessings. What you need more than any of those things if you are to meet life's challenges head on, what you must acquire if it doesn't come naturally to you, is the right attitude.

By the right attitude I mean, of course, not whining. No one likes a whiner. The worst sort of whiner has no friends or career prospects. The best sort has no friends. What's more, a lifetime of whining turns you so mean and ugly that when you are fifty-five, children will throw stones at you in the street.

Happily you were born with nothing to whine about and so far none of you has moaned unusually often, but there is a tendency to poor thinking on your father's side. Since poor thinking is a near relative of the whine and since these things can creep up on you, as can be seen in the way I now look like my mother in my underwear, I don't think we can be complacent. Incorrect thinking may be lurking on the very fringe of your future behaviour.

YOUR FATHER

Your father is not a whiner. He stops short of whining because he has a stout heart and likes a laugh, but we all know he can spot a cloud on any old silver lining and that this causes him misery which is only interesting sometimes. He believes this tendency is constitutional. Either something he eats or something in the blood. But my argument is if it's food, he owes it to the world to starve, and if it's in the blood, he doesn't have a leg to stand on. What's in the blood is no excuse for anything.

Once you are twenty-five you are no longer entitled to blame your parents for what you are. Once you are twenty-five, you choose to be what you are. Even if whining is embedded in your DNA like nuts in nougat, you can and must resist it. That is what life is. An endless tussle with nature's and nurture's least wanted gifts. I am continuing to struggle with my exhibitionism, as you know.

By curbing and resisting the dreadful inclinations we a) are born with and b) learn in our youth, we become better human beings, move on to a higher plane and get to choose what we will come back as in the next life, if we subscribe to the notion of a next life. This is what Buddha said. Or someone he knew. He said positive thinking means taking life as it comes, appreciating what you have, making considered choices and understanding there is no such thing as total control. Well, someone did. It doesn't matter who. It is correct thinking.

But

'But . . .' I hear you say and I welcome *but*. You must keep *but* on the tip of your tongues at all times for it leads to the area of grey in which we battle not only with nature and nurture but the whole human conundrum. '*But*,' you are thinking: what if your father has clinical depression plummeting down his family tree and smashing into his head rendering him incapable of happiness. Very good. An excellent *but*. It brings me to a fine example of correct thinking.

Correct thinking in the presence of a clinical tendency to misery: 'Tough.' There's nothing wrong with a little bit of misery that a few trips to the shrink and maybe some medication can't fix.

Got a problem you can't fix? Get help. Help, under any circumstances, should be resorted to with only a modicum of hesitation. A little mad? Find a doctor. So, with mental illness out of the equation, how can a daughter, who isn't born with it, acquire correct thinking?

Looking on the bright side

Under no circumstances must you be permanently glad in the mode of Pollyanna who was a dim wit. Permanent gladness is unnatural and foolhardy. Permanently glad people who are always looking on the bright side will not only one day be arrested, they will be caught off guard by people knifing them in the back and by the small print in loan documents.

Look on the bright side by all means, but look even longer and harder at the seamy side. There is positively no one to blame but yourself if schemes and dreams

collapse owing to your own failure to take everything
into account. I draw your attention to a troubling
incident from my own life.

AN INCIDENT FROM MY OWN LIFE

My first novel was about a girl who grew a penis and I
wrote it during my third pregnancy. I don't know why.
Linda, a few blocks down the road with the daughter
your age who moved to America, typed it up for me
and she liked it. I didn't know what to make of it. I was
pregnant. But my agent at the time adored it. She said it
was a work of genius and the find of her career. Maybe
she was pregnant too.

The agent was so confident about this book that she
came round one evening to talk to your father and me
about how we would deal with the success she was
certain would hit us like a whirlwind. I couldn't think
of a title but she said it didn't matter. It had everything
going for it and she was going to auction it. So your
father and I sat back and waited to be covered in glory.

She sent the book out to selected publishers and the
selected publishers, appalled at her shamelessness, sent
it back. It was a total wash-out. I immediately leaked
rhesus negative blood into the baby's rhesus positive
blood and thought I'd never write again. But the baby
survived and so did I.

What I learnt was correct thinking for dreams and
schemes. Hope for everything but expect nothing. It is a
balanced outlook that goes hand in hand with a sense
of proportion.

A SENSE OF PROPORTION

This is the cornerstone of all correct thinking. There are two strategies for acquiring it. The first, hoping without expecting, rules out overreacting which is embarrassing and useless as you will gather from the above. There's nothing wrong with hope. We wouldn't move without it. Always hope. But know in your heart and soul that anything can go wrong at any time and mostly does.

EXAMPLES FROM YOUR EVERYDAY LIFE

You lose your purse. Say you lose your purse again. You say, 'Please, God, let Pollyanna find it and return it to me,' but you don't expect her to so you will get on with the dreary, crapola business of replacing everything. This is nature's punishment for carelessness and totally acceptable. Correct thinking in the event of a purse loss is, 'It's gone. I will accept my lot. I will spare my father's feelings by not telling him.'

You get your hair cut. You hope to look like Cathérine Deneuve. You look like Danny de Vito. You think correctly: Aaah! Then you let it go. Hair grows. You always looked more like Danny de Vito anyway.

You go for a job. You hope to get it. Some der-brain does. Correct thinking: it wasn't the job for me since I am not a der-brain. Soon I will get the job that is for me. Meantime, I will submerge myself in my art and work hard at a job which is beneath me just to show the kind of girl I am.

The joy in hoping but not expecting is that you

are always prepared for any eventuality. It keeps
disappointment to a minimum. And this is my heart's
desire. To spare you disappointment. A little bit is fine.
Too much is too much.

When life's progress involves so much bouncing
back, it is folly to give yourself too huge a bounce
to make. Hoping but not expecting also puts a
curb on kidding yourself which is pitifully incorrect
thinking. You need look no further than the
Royal family.

KEEPING YOUR FEET ON THE GROUND

The second strategy is a threefold job: assess,
attack, accept. It works like this. You get dumped.
Say some boy dumps you, breaks your heart
and you see no way out of your misery. You
sing many mournful songs but it's no use. You
hope to get him back. You don't really expect
to because he caught you snogging his best
friend. But you hope. What's the point in that?
Hoping on its own will get you nowhere. You
have to act.

First assess: to wade in or not to wade in? What
kind of wade in? There will be the usual possibilities-
sobbing down the phone with hiccoughs, getting friends
to say you are on a life support machine, sucking
up to his mother. You size them up. You may
go for one or all the options or you may decide the
situation is beyond hope and walk away from it once
and for all.

Whatever, you act on your decision and having
acted, you accept the outcome. Acceptance of an
outcome is correct thinking. You give something your

best shot then you accept the result knowing you can do no more.

REGULAR MISERY

What happens, you will be wanting to know, if you are very, very disappointed, betrayed and hurt, even by an outcome you have been expecting and prepared for? What is correct thinking then? It is this. Be as miserable as you like. But keep it short.

By and large, misery is not irredeemable. It's a passing thing and everyone is prone to it occasionally if they aren't psychotic. Only weirdos go through life without having their hearts broken over something.

The correct thinking with a broken heart is to know it's broken and to off-load the pain wherever and whenever you can. Only by off-loading can you return to regular functioning. You may off-load by the truck-full on those closest to you but soon they will tell you to shut up. You then off-load in little seepy bits on strangers at bus stops or in the post office. This is acceptable and restores a sense of proportion.

Off-loading is not to be confused with whining which is unacceptable at every level. Whiners whine and fail to act or accept. They say 'I can't' but mean 'I won't'. They are terrible people. Very often they are passive aggressive which is to say they wield power with their weakness. Whatever you do, don't marry one.

Incorrect thinking isn't as bad as whining but it can lead to obsessive/compulsive behaviour, debilitation, circles under the eyes and too much hand-washing.

Adopt correct thinking and contentment will be your middle name.

Rule: Never auction a book without a title.

EARLY
LEARNING

THE SECRET OF
A GOOD EDUCATION

I had to send you to school even though I knew what
it would be like. One, it's against the law not to go
until you are sixteen. And two, you need the grades to
get to a decent university. You may not want to go to
university but you don't want to find you can't because
you didn't pass the right exams. You want the choice.
Choice, you will discover, is central to happiness. That's
why having none is the worst punishment in the world.
That and deprivation of liberty. But look at me, talking
about jail when I'm thinking of school.

I sometimes wonder whether my hating it has
scarred you for life. I like to imagine I've taken a
balanced and enthusiastic approach to your education
and chosen schools that, with one notable exception,
have served you well. But it could be argued I've
been overvigilant in my response to gross injustice,
professional incompetence and horrible girls. Maybe it
could. I don't know by whom.

Moral support

As far as I'm concerned parents should support the school they have chosen for their children but only to a point. And they should be circumspect in response to ugliness in the playground because playgrounds are just ugly. But there will be times when a mother should intervene and cry, 'Get away from her, you pigs' in no uncertain terms. If you think I have retarded your development in any way, just say so but not to me. I thought I was acting in your best interests.

Grim experiences

What would you have done about that girl who shoved one of you off the stage in the school play? She was ringleading a bullying campaign that ran over many months and took years off my life. I accosted her in a dark corner, grabbed her by the bicep, squeezed hard and told her to back off or else. 'Or else!' I hissed. She cried in fright but was otherwise unmoved. I approached her parents who told me she was a bed-wetter. In the end I reported her to the teacher and after that she backed off.

And when there was the gross injustice in the art department I reported the art teacher. The rigging of exam results saw one of your places plummet from near the top to near the bottom so I was down to the school with my briefcase and on to the education department so quickly no one knew what had hit them. Not even me. Justice was done, however.

I haven't intervened nearly as often as I'd have liked, but what I want you to learn from me sticking my oar in is that I will support you against any person or system which threatens to overwhelm you any time, any place and that you should never be frightened of taking them on yourself. The truth is that whatever a mother says or does, school is mainly a scarring experience which is as it should be. To send a child into the world uncalloused is a cruel and unnatural punishment.

Knowing this is no consolation while you're at school, I accept that. There are so many causes for frustration, discontent and misery that it has to be unbearable at times. When this occurs, the temptation is to withdraw into yourself and imagine acts of violence. It is more productive to make lists. There should be two: one in favour of school and the other against. They might include any of the following:

THE CASE AGAINST SCHOOL

It goes on and on
I'm doing badly
I can't stand the stress
Homework is mad
The whole thing is pointless
I hate the teachers
They hate me
I have no friends
The food is disgusting
Sport is humiliating

IN FAVOUR

It ends
Good exam results will keep my options open

Excellent teachers (name them)
Enjoyable lessons (name them)
Decent lunches (name them)
Decent friends (at least one)
The bus
Talking about the weekend

The fact that the against list is longer than the in favour
represents a personal bias. There will be many more
things in favour which I just can't recall from my own
experience. When you have looked at the lists you must
crumple them up and throw them away. The point of
the exercise is to articulate the source of your misery,
not dwell on it. But I have one or two observations to
make which you may find helpful.

THE REALITY

It isn't anyone's fault. The problem with school is in the
nature of the beast. At its worst, it's having to spend
long hours doing stuff you'd never ever choose to do in
the company of a whole lot of people you'd prefer never
to see again.

You could be educated by yourself at home and
wander freely from subject to subject as your fancy
took you and maybe you would become an intellectual
giant. But you would also be a social retard and since
I am the mother and it's my choice, I have opted for
social aptitude. You are all much better at making
friends than I was. You even get to keep them.

At its best, school is fun and even inspirational.
You all know a lot about art history, I must say. And
although I say I hated school, I wasn't consumed by

misery all the time. There were minutes, hours, days, even weeks that were OK.

I was a terrible student and almost completely incapable of paying attention which led to disruptive behaviour and exclusion from the classroom. Once outside I spent many a happy hour dodging the nuns who patrolled the corridors to see who was standing in them. And sometimes I had friends. There was a very nice dog who hung around the lower tennis court. And also Jessie the lady who sold sweets. I was a sad individual and I think possibly bitter.

You are all far too pretty and well-dressed to be sads. And you have no real reason to be bitter. What's more, there is so much more point to school now. In my day there was full employment and to do badly in exams wasn't the body blow to choice it is today. You could skive and I did. For you the pressure is well and truly on.

Your schools set you huge amounts of work and expect you to get it done which, mostly, you do and this is what we are paying for. It may be extremely stressful but you are learning mental discipline and I can assure you that this will stand you in excellent stead for the rest of your life, as well as for passing exams.

WHY YOU SHOULDN'T TAKE A LEAF OUT OF MY BOOK

I had a personality problem. I couldn't stand not to feel involved and in the sixties there was no question of involving pupils in the lessons. Dialogue was out of the question. The teacher spoke. You did uninvited and you died. After a while you stopped listening and either nodded off or mucked about and soon you became known as someone who nodded off or mucked about. Then, any little thing was enough to provoke.

THE TIME I ASKED ABOUT PI

In the maths lesson on pi, for instance, I put up my hand to ask the simple question, 'Why is pi?' The nun giving the lesson had given the same one on pi for thirty years and it brooked no interruption. I was out of that class for rudeness before you could say Jack Robinson. That was the kind of schooling I had.

You, on the other hand, are a joy to teach because you are so active in class discussions. That's what they say. As a consequence, there have always been classes that you have enjoyed and teachers you've liked and none of you has ever been threatened with expulsion. This makes me very proud. I put it down to progress in education and the quality of your characters for which I claim some credit.

COWS WHO BULLY

What hasn't changed is the playground. There were always girls who were cows and now there are many more. Usually they befriend other cows to form a herd and from the security of this herd they launch attacks on unsuspecting individuals who want only to be their friends or left alone. Sometimes in their herd there will be girls who aren't cows but who aren't game enough to say so.

Bullying is now a national sport and only the rare cow or invisible person is safe from it. You will attract it if you are in any way different or if it's your turn.

Mostly it will take the form of insults, running away, ganging up, nicking your lunch, laughing at you behind your back and sneering, all of which amounts to rejection. It can last for hours or years.

It's well known that looking as if you care will only make it worse. I don't know how you are supposed to look as if you don't care unless it's by becoming a cow yourself, and I suppose that's an option, but it's not the best one. The best one is to tell yourself they are slugs under stones and you have no intention of stooping to their level. I'd rather feel lonely than like a piece of slime any day.

The best protection is a group of loyal friends but a very low premium is put on loyalty in the average playground; it's every woman for herself when it comes to a place in the pecking order. I want you to know that because I have encouraged you to go your own way and ignore the herd, your misery is my misery. You might think that had it not been for my misery, you would have no misery but I would rather you didn't.

My consolation is that although you have all been miserable from time to time, you seem to cope well and have people to talk to whom you like. If ever it gets bad, however, ring me, I'll get a few friends together and we'll get down to the school and kick bottom.

THE SECRET OF SCHOOL

The best way to survive school is to treat it for what it is. A centre of learning. Most of what you learn in the classroom you will forget. You will, however, remember most importantly how to stick at tasks you hate, how to use your brain when it badly wants to rest, how to mix with people you detest, how to survive a system which can be brutal and how to rise to challenges of an unpalatable nature. These are proper lessons for life and you will do well to learn them thoroughly as I believe I did.

Rule: Pi is 3.1416 but no one knows why.

How to make
a good impression

As my agent likes to say, and he, I believe, is quoting Krishna, you only get one go at a first impression. This implies that an impression once formed is devilishly hard to budge and I think he's right.

This is why you must never allow a whine so much as to enter your head, let alone your voice or expression, and you must get your grooming right first up (see Grooming). It's also why you must be scrupulous about hygiene and smell. Very often, you will be smelt before you are seen.

SMELL

Should you find yourself approaching the person you are wishing to impress from behind and you are in a pub or on the Tube, the chances are that you will smell like your surroundings or the person next to you. Make every effort to dissociate yourself from this smell by going, 'Pugh! What's that pong?'

Do not attempt to overwhelm with your own body odour, be it natural or enhanced, because this will involve either standing too close to the person you are wishing to impress or having to wear so much enhancement that when you reach fresh air that person will be forced to flee. Your own scent should always be subtle. But recognisable.

WHICH SCENT

While I am a great advocate of ringing the changes in most aspects of physical presentation, I hold the view that you should cultivate a scent that is your own. It doesn't matter who invented it, find one that you can live with that doesn't cause widespread offence and stick to it for a decent period. That way, if you have made a good first impression, you will be off to a flying start when it comes to the second, third and fourth. Also, should you ever find yourself involved in espionage, you can disguise your first impression by changing scents. You cannot lay down the groundwork too early for a job with the Foreign Office.

SMILE

The most important reason for smiling when you wish to make a good impression is to put an end to any confusion that your natural expression is one of infinite sourness or, in our case, idiocy. The women in our family have, sadly, all been born with slack jaws which are inclined to give us away in moments of intense concentration. Make sure your smile doesn't compound this felony.

Do not smile too often or too long. It's our natural tendency and an unhappy one. Smile on introduction and after that only when the impressee is smiling. This will indicate not only that you are companionable but that you are on their wavelength. After you have made a good first impression, you can smile if and when you please.

ARM TOUCHING

This much abused tactic used to be a quick indication of warmth and affection or at least kind feelings. Unfortunately it is now imbued with sexual interest and overfamiliarity so use it sparingly.

WHICH IMPRESSION

Having impressed with your smell and your smile and not offended with careless or inappropriate grooming or overfamiliarity you must then tailor your behaviour. What it is you want to achieve? A job? A date? Your money back? There are a squillion and one instances of first impressions and as many possible outcomes.

Some you can manoeuvre with clever personality changes. Some you can't because the person you are trying to impress has already formed an impression without having met you. We call these people jerks.

They may turn out to be OK on second, third or fiftieth meeting but you will be lumbered with their preconceptions at the first and there's not much you can do about it. Let me refer you to some everyday situations.

BOYFRIENDS' FAMILIES

Sooner or later you will be introduced to the family of a special boyfriend. How well I remember coming off the plane to meet my eldest brother-in-law for the first time. I was wearing a very nice ecru mini skirt, my hair in a long ponytail and quite enough make-up to suggest that even if I was nineteen and from Australia, I knew how people looked abroad. 'Ah,' boomed your uncle, 'your teeth aren't nearly as big as I thought they were.'

That old smile problem again. Had I not smiled so long and so hard in the photographs sent home by your father, who knows what he would have said.

By and large, families of boyfriends want you to look normal, sound normal and not have criminal records. They don't want trouble in the way of opinions they don't recognise, manners that challenge theirs or any suggestion that you are in it for the money. The less fixed the impression the better, with boyfriends' families.

EMPLOYERS

No matter how important the job you are applying for, prospective employers want intelligence without arrogance and confidence without brashness. They want to know you can work without supervision yet not run off with the petty cash, that you can function in a team without being subversive, and that you won't frighten the punters. They like good hair, skin and teeth. You can manage all of this. You can.

Some prospective employers are difficult and ugly people who delight in giving applicants a hard time. May they rot in hell. But most will want to like you because they want the post filled. Never look desperate. Always be prepared to turn the job down. Avoid offering too much understanding. Arm touching is not good here although it can make an excellent first impression when you are visiting the elderly in hospital where it is unlikely to be considered sexually provocative.

MASSIVE CHALLENGES

There are situations that are so tricky that being able to enter them at all, let alone function intelligently within them, is a massive challenge. This can include approaching people of whom you are in awe (hold the smile, ask if they know your sister), voicing an unpopular opinion (smile, say you have a sister who agrees with you), and singing, speaking and taking your clothes off in public, which will only crop up together should you choose to enter Miss World.

If I were you, I wouldn't enter Miss World. Doing so will create an impression that will stay with you for the rest of your life. When you become Madame Speaker in the House of Commons, profiles of you will always begin, 'Former Miss World' as you would undoubtedly win and people will think you didn't have a brain.

On the question of performing in public at all, you will do well to avoid it if the very thought makes you lose your lunch. It does, however, get easier with practice, or so I am told. At your first attempt, approach it as if you were someone else.

Think yourself into the kind of character who performs in public all the time, dress as this person, smile as this person, stand up as this person, and be that person. Then if you are a disaster you can blame that person.

You can, alternatively, prepare yourself by imagining yourself in the situation, thinking yourself through every minute of the situation and seeing yourself triumph. That is also supposed to work. It never has for me but this could be lack of focus.

Another tactic is to take immense pleasure in the moment. Imagine neither success nor failure, stay within your own body and take it a second at a time, revelling in the attention you are getting. I read somewhere Margot Fonteyn liked that one and she went places.

GRATUITOUS RUDENESS

People will always call rudeness gratuitous but it rarely is. Nearly always it's provoked by other people being gratuitously rude to you. On the occasion of someone else's gratuitous rudeness, it is perfectly correct to give the impression of a woman who can defend herself verbally and if necessary with her bag. But it isn't always wise. You may blow your chances, whatever they were, with displays of untoward strength which will be put down to aggression. It is for you to decide the odds.

There are tactics for ignoring rudeness. One is to treat it as a test of your mettle and to produce your mettle at its finest. As in: 'You may be right but she is in other respects a perfectly competent mother.' To dig deep within yourself and find calm when agitation is expected is a deeply rewarding and happy experience. You don't want to dig too often, however, or you will get cancer.

A SINGULAR FAILURE TO IMPRESS
FROM MY OWN LIFE

It's a sad and sorry truth that some people will take a dislike to us, wish us harm and not shy from doing us harm. You will recognise these people because they will stare at you in a funny and menacing way even though they are with people who like you. This isn't paranoia. What's paranoia if it isn't intuition?

Husbands of friends have often taken a dislike to me, usually on the grounds of my emotional coldness and/or poor behaviour. Once, at a restaurant, the man on my left said he had to tell me, he really did have to, that he had never liked me. What's more, he disliked me more every time we met. He watched my behaviour and it disgusted him. I set out to provoke. I fixed on some poor devil in my company and I made this poor devil's night a misery with my taunting. I was disgusting.

I had, with this man, not only failed with the first impression but on every successive impression. What can I tell you? It happens. Creep!

YOUR GRANDFATHER

I counsel you to remember all the above but also to bear in mind what your maternal grandfather said most days after a Scotch or eight. 'Always be yourself.' The best impression you will make is when you aren't trying to be something you're not, despite my advice on performing in public. Since you are all, at heart, among the very finest that human nature has to offer, I can't imagine anyone thinking you are much short of perfect. On first acquaintance. And if they do, they will be very much mistaken.

Rule: *The friends of friends are only occasionally people you want to see again. Their husbands are even stranger.*

MANNERS

Do manners maketh the man? Does it matter? It does. Manners are the method by which you will be identified. You can say as much as you like, 'Hey – people should take me as they find me,' but the real question is, 'What do I want to be taken for?' A woman who eats like a pig? I don't think so.

What I want you to be taken for, and I am your mother so it counts, are women who care at least a little about the comfort of others. This means having some empathy, as well as sympathy; having a little bit of consideration.

It means not shovelling your food, not pushing in front of people in doorways, always saying please and thank you, not pinching your girlfriends' boyfriends and watching your tongue. As a result of my dismal tendency to show off and not watch my tongue, my own manners can be a little rickety. This is no excuse for you, however.

It helps, I think, to separate manners from courtesy. Manners will identify your social background but they only sometimes have anything to do with courtesy.

EATING

This is my point. Eat like a pig and only some people will go, 'Ah, a woman who eats like a pig.' In this country, it is really only members of the middle class who insist their children eat with their mouths closed, never speak when eating and chew silently.

Everyone else makes a point of chewing as noisily as possible and exposing to the general view the progress of this chewing. It makes me, for one, want to throw up. All that saliva and snuffling. My aversion could have something to do with having been brought up in a country which calls itself classless. Or it could just be a weak stomach. I do know that my mother had very specific ideas about courteous behaviour, at the table and elsewhere, and so did the nuns.

AT THE TABLE

Aside from not chewing like a horse, you keep your elbows off the table but as far as possible from the ribs of the people on either side. You hold your knife and fork properly, gripped firmly, not as if they were pencils, and you keep them on your plate except when they are being lifted to your mouth. You never reach across, you ask to have things passed, you don't push your food around your plate, and you only take the last helping when you are sure no one else wants it, even if it's your sister; then you share. If you share, you don't squabble over whose bit is biggest. If your sister's manners are upsetting you, you don't glare, tut and make projectile vomiting noises. You keep your eyes on your plate, just as you would if you were out, unless you are answering or asking a question and there is no food in your mouth.

Don't curl your little finger when you raise a glass or cup to your lip. It isn't bad manners but people will laugh.

WHAT? PARDON?

Table manners are for the consideration of others but they are also aids to digestion. Other manners have no element of consideration but are for tribal identification. Like saying 'What?' or 'Pardon?' As expressions go, neither has much to recommend it. 'What' sounds rude and peremptory and 'Pardon' sounds weedy with a bit of whine. 'What did you say?' or 'I beg your pardon' is better. Even 'Sorry' is better. But provided you look intelligent and interested, who cares?

If you elect to use what or pardon, you will be identified as belonging or aspiring to one class or another. However, your accent will give you away just as surely and so will a whole lot of other stuff like knowing when the shooting season begins and whether to spend the summer in Scotland.

You can't dismiss completely the notion of manners which are for identification purposes only. They come in handy in the area of forming friendships view marriage. You're more likely to share hopes and values with people from a similar background. But this isn't always true. Courtesy which is based on consideration for others is far more important.

COURTESY

It begins with please and thank you, as well as
not pushing, and involves not only consideration,
but appreciation of others and sublimation of self.
Deferring is no longer fashionable. Not to one's
elders. Not to anyone. I, for one, don't mourn its
passing in my personal life, though it seems to me
that many structures are the poorer for it since it
hasn't been replaced with any noticeable acceptance of
responsibility. Respect is a different matter.

Respect should be shown at all times to everyone
until they give you reason not to extend it. Particular
attention should be paid to the elderly who know much
more than you, have much to tell you but who may
be a little deaf. You may be afflicted with deafness
one day and find for yourself how frustrating it is to
have something to say but no real way of knowing
when is the time to say it. Never be impatient with the
hard of hearing. Unless it's your father and he is only
pretending.

Always offer your seat on a train or bus to the
elderly, infirm or pregnant. Stare pointedly at everyone
who doesn't.

Appreciation for hospitality must always be offered.
This means showing pleasure in the cooking, which
mustn't be excessive or grovelling, note-writing, phone
calls or flowers to express thanks, and offering to
help. Always offer to help clear the table and with the
washing up, though not if you are in a restaurant.

GIFTS

Should you take a present when you go on holiday or to stay with friends? Not necessarily. It depends on how old you are and who the friends are. If you are at school and invited away with the friend of a family, a gift is a good idea and I would give it at the beginning of the visit so your hosts don't spend the whole of your time with them indulging you and thinking what a mean git you are. If you are earning, the decent thing is to take your hosts out for a meal.

Sometimes a precedent has already been established, however. You might have had the friend to stay and he or she has come without a gift or the slightest inclination to take you out for a meal. In that case, don't cause embarrassment by showing them up with your own generosity. Just offer much help and ask yourself how badly you want to keep seeing them.

PUNCTUALITY

Punctuality is a matter of organisation and a gift of nature. To be punctual in your business life is essential. Always telephone if you are going to be more than five minutes late. Socially, it's different. To be ten minutes late was fashionable and considered correct for a very long time. Now guests can be up to an hour late and not feel the need to apologise. This drives me nuts.

If you are asked to arrive between seven thirty and eight, telephone if you are to be later than eight fifteen. If you are meeting someone on a street corner, twenty minutes is as long as you need to hang about. After that you may be arrested for soliciting. Never leave a dinner party before the pudding unless you have given notice, and you ought only to leave before coffee if it is unbearably late or you are bored to sobs and never wish to see your hosts again.

AN UNPUNCTUAL MOMENT WHEN I WAS PREGNANT WHICH WAS NO EXCUSE

When I was expecting our third baby, before the terrible incident with the untitled book, we were asked to lunch by friends who had also invited a cricketer I was longing to meet. The cricketer was in his seventies and the meal was to be early. We were asked for eleven. The house where we were expected was a ninety-minute drive away.

I don't know what got into me. A baby, but what else? Despite your father urging me to get a move on, I couldn't get myself ready until eleven. I kept saying no one ate before one. By the time we arrived – at one – lunch was over. Everyone was furious and no one cared I was pregnant.

The moral of this story is house rules prevail. If the host says get there at eleven, he means get there at eleven or bugger off.

MY OWN MANNERS

I always regret my lapses in the courtesy department. Many's the time I have left the note-writing until it's too late to write yet composed something exquisite over and over in my head to compensate. How often have I spat food across the table into the lap of the person opposite in my excitement to make a point? It is worse now I am

afflicted with middle-aged dribble. But knowing how to
behave is what counts.

This leads me to another piece of advice. Should
anyone who isn't your sister disgust you, the
same rules apply as if this person was your sister.
You must not make any unseemly noise or betray
by any expression on your face that you want
to be ill.

ANOTHER INCIDENT FROM MY LIFE

I don't believe I ever behaved better than the time
a world famous author spat directly into my mouth.
He was reading to me from his latest book, my jaw
was suitably dropped and my mouth agape with
interest, when he said something beginning with S
and middle-aged dribble shot from his mouth and
into mine.

What could I do? Certainly I couldn't swallow or
close my mouth. Spitting was out of the question.
Speaking intelligibly was impossible. So I spoke
unintelligibly which was enough for him as he
was more interested in what he had to say than in
anything I might. When he was obliged to take a
phone call several minutes later, I relieved myself into
a handkerchief. I often tell this story in my honour
to show how well one can conduct oneself during
conversation.

RUDENESS AT CERTAIN AGES

There are two stages in your development when you will be rude because you feel entitled. One is between the ages of thirteen and twenty-three; the other is from seventy onwards. All that differs is who you are rude to.

From thirteen to twenty-three, you feel entitled to be rude to other family members because you know they are ganging up on you and getting at you because they hate you. Your response is to yell, slam doors, curse and make angry gestures with your arms and legs. A little of this goes a long way. In our family I have become more tolerant with every passing daughter. I now see that it is a terrible thing to be treated like a baby when you are no longer a baby and that you should be accorded adult respect although it is unfamiliar. I also understand it is important for offspring to make themselves a little repellant in order to separate from a clinging and overprotective mother. That's OK, but watch it. My feelings can tolerate only so much. After a bit, I want an apology.

In your late teens and early twenties, it is also easy to be ruder than intended to the outside world because you imagine the outside world is not taking you seriously. When I was a very young reporter, aged no more than seventeen, I was so grand with people I was interviewing that one kind-hearted photographer couldn't stand to work with me. Yikes, I think now about that period.

Once you are seventy, you can be as rude as you like to anyone because you no longer care about making a good impression. This is a mistake. You will soon become the neighbourhood's mad old lady who lives by herself and is mistaken for a witch. Children will whimper when they pass you in the street and you will have hairs on your chin because you care too little to pluck them out.

SOCIAL INTERCOURSE

I am frequently criticised for my overexcitement in social intercourse. It leads to speaking louder than everyone else and across everyone else. I accept this can be trying but my argument is that at least I'm showing an interest.

There are manners for polite conversation: don't interrupt, don't speak across, don't hog the floor, don't be sullen. You can ignore these when everyone is having a good time. There are, in my book, only two rules you should always abide by. The first is never to say, 'You're wrong.' Someone is only ever wrong in your opinion. And you must never imagine you are being asked about yourself because you are interesting. You are being asked about yourself out of courtesy. You must show equal interest back.

This is how conversations should go: you ask about me; I ask about you; you tell a story; I tell a story; you venture an opinion; I venture mine; you comment on mine; I comment on yours. If someone rings up and says, 'My cat's died,' the correct response is not, 'I don't have a cat.'

There are always times when conversations will be unequal. But in the general course of meeting people, it is a thug who doesn't show curiosity. Should you find yourself in the company of a thug, it is perfectly reasonable for you to say, 'I am leaving now because you are a bore.'

So there you are. Manners are dictated by courtesy and conversation by curiosity. Now you will always

know how to behave when you're out even if you've
never read Nancy Mitford.

Rule: Always carry a handkerchief. Spit can come from
anywhere.

CULTURE

Culture is somewhere between manners and education. You don't have to have it but it's jolly nice if you do; your mind will be broader, your outlook more informed and in time people older than you will respect you as a surprisingly well rounded and refined person, given who your parents are.

That's what culture is: a refined understanding of all things arty farty, in this country as well as abroad. To acquire it and be known for it, you should travel widely, familiarising yourself with local food, wine and little known dialects; you should read widely, mainly the subtexts; listen to and memorise music of all sorts, especially any accompaniment on native instruments; go to concerts and operas; visit art galleries; get to the theatre and immerse yourself in at least one ancient language and civilisation plus a little pottery. But frankly, who has the time? Who has the money?

Usually it's enough to read the reviews, master a few foreign phrases which you can use ironically and mix with informed people. The impression of culture is almost as good as culture itself and it's all most people manage.

SPECIALISE

I would strongly counsel pursuing at least one branch
of the arts about which you can speak knowledgeably,
or if not knowledgeably, enticingly. You don't have to
be an expert, just enthusiastic. I have chosen country
music and daily newspapers but I have a reasonable
smattering of English, American and Australian
literature, a little opera and some art from the
Renaissance onwards. I say some. I mean none but it
doesn't stop me talking about it.

Culture for most people is seventy per cent bluffing,
twenty-five per cent genuine interest and five per cent
knowledge. This is a happy circumstance since almost
no one can catch anyone out with any real certainty.

A WARNING FROM MY OWN LIFE

It is important, however, never to use a name or
cultural reference unless you can pronounce it. I was
caught short in W.H. Smiths when I first asked for
a work by Goethe whose real name is Gerter. Also,
be wary of ostentatiously beating time in orchestral
concerts. The rhythm changes bewilderingly mid-phrase
and you can be left patting waltz time when it's
suddenly six-eight. Is that what I mean? Is there such a
thing as six-eight? You are the musical ones.

Go to Florence as often as possible and learn to
speak Italian from one of those audio tapes. That will
set you up for life.

Rule: *Rheims, site of the famous cathedral, is pronounced Rance as in rancid with a little bit less n.*

GRACE IN THE FACE
OF UNPLEASANT NOISES
AND SO ON

I haven't mentioned grace, yet you should acquire it even before refinement as it is a transcending quality which will enable you to rise above many awkward moments. It doesn't come naturally to me which is a crying shame. In this case, you must do as I say and not as I do.

By grace, I mean easy and sensitive behaviour in the face of adversity when loud, brash and unpleasant behaviour will only embarrass everyone. Loud, brash and unpleasant is home ground for me, as is the coarse and profane route through social handicap.

Don't for a minute imagine I am incapable of feeling silly. I just pretend I am to make myself feel better. Perhaps you will work at grace if you understand how badly I have wanted it.

AN ANECDOTE ILLUSTRATING STUPID
THEN LOUD

When I first came to London aged nineteen, I was given some casual work on the news desk of the *Mirror* which was in those days a proud newspaper. I was given one story only, about a woman from Boulogne who was doubly incontinent. Maybe it was a joke. How was I to know? I was new. I thought Boulogne was pronounced Bologna and I didn't know what incontinent was.

I said to the man next to me, 'Where is Bologna?' He said, 'Italy.' Then I said, 'What is doubly incontinent?' He said, 'Well, you know singly incontinent?' I thought I was writing about an Italian woman with two passports. And that's not all. In my confusion, I spotted a familiar face across the newsroom, a subeditor from Australia whom I greeted with a gusto that took his breath away. I talked to him with such animation, he could only stand it for three minutes. When he backed away, I was so overcome by emotion that I turned to a senior reporter who had been watching us distractedly and cried affectionately, 'What are you looking at, silly bitch?' She didn't know it was affection. She never spoke to me again.

This is a wretched story. Every time I think about it, I pray for grace.

SHOULD YOUR KNICKERS FALL DOWN

I should have some because your grandmother has. When she was a young woman she would walk to work along a very busy road in the middle of the city. One day, on her walk, she found that the elastic in her knickers had snapped and the knickers were wending their way towards her knees. She tried to jam them between her thighs but she had many blocks to go and this was determined underwear. She entered a store with two adjacent entrances, stepped out of the knickers in one doorway and left by the other without so much as a downward glance. That is grace.

NOISES

I have told you before about the wind crisis during my third pregnancy. I wrote about it once and received a letter of outrage from a woman who wanted to know what was so clever about describing bodily functions for public consumption. That woman will be shot through with grace.

I'll tell you again just in case my position improves with the telling. In the latter stages of my last pregnancy, I was cruelly overtaken by wind. There wasn't a thing I could do about it. Clenching everything failed. Avoiding gaseous foods was a complete waste of time. One night, we had to go to a dinner party but I thought I would be all right if I didn't move very much. This was madness. As I reached for the pepper, the sound of a punctured feral balloon escaped me.

'I'm sorry,' I said. 'That was me.' Everyone stared hard at their plates. Embarrassed by the silence, I spoke up with verve and candour. 'That was me, that noise,' I said. No one spoke. For the third time I said, 'Ha! Just farted!' And when I was ignored for the third time I came to understand that the graceful thing would have been to ignore it myself. Pregnant women are like the Queen and assumed to be above bodily functions.

The same does not apply to non-pregnant women. Then a simple excuse would suffice rather

than a prolonged explanation. Laughing like a
drain is out.

I would like to offer many more suggestions for
graceful behaviour but they are not within my gift.
Would that they were. Walking quickly and smiling into
mid-distance would seem to work for most things.

*Rule: In the event of falling over, any of the following
are acceptable: a) crying; b) pretending to be knocked
unconscious; c) leaping to your feet and glaring at a fixed
point on the ground. Do not scream or laugh like a hyena.*

SHOWING OFF

Here are ten things you need to know about showing off which is widely considered to be a social handicap:

1. Not everyone will laugh.
2. In full flight, you won't care.
3. If the audience is looking ugly, pretend to be drunk.
4. Two show-offs at one table is one show-off too many.
5. Only stand on a chair if you know what you are going to do once you're up there.
6. Vary your act – especially one that usually involves tricks.
7. Keep your clothes on.
8. Accents are dangerous. Especially anything Welsh or Indian which both sound Welsh or Indian.
9. Get down from the chair if more than one person throws something at you.
10. Only apologise next day if you broke something.

Rule: *Never get a laugh by interrupting someone else's anecdote, especially if I am that someone.*

FEMALE
WILES

GROOMING

Never think you are so stylish you can neglect your grooming. On this I am with your grandmother who believes it suggests breeding. Or perhaps it's the other way round. In any case, it's her opinion and mine that a well groomed woman looks as if she knows what it's all about and is going places. Your grandmother thinks it can be achieved by and large with a hairbrush and an iron. I think it's more a matter of well-considered projection but first, a word on tattoos.

No.

Especially Chinese symbols, butterflies and signs of the zodiac. They are as fascinating as ginger lip gloss and they don't have lip gloss's valuable vanishing properties. Go for *I love you Mum* if you must but before committing yourself to life as the kind of hard girl who can stand pain as well as something wacky on her buttock, think again.

THAT WOMAN AT THE AIRPORT

Think about that big woman we saw at the airport. She was sixty-four if she was a day, had a huge tattoo of a dragon on her arm, a Marks and Sparks summer frock, Dr Scholl sandals, a perm and she looked bananas. Total style confusion.

Once she would have been a beatnik. But the beatnik will grow into the matron just as the punk will grow into the chartered accountant. You can never guarantee the requirements of your changing look so don't lumber yourself with permanent expressions from a former life. Especially when your future life could involve Dr Scholl sandals.

The point about self-adornment is the fun you have adapting it to suit your circumstances. Nothing will cheer you up as much as a haircut that says drop dead. Or a little bit of body piercing. Which is reversible.

PROJECTION

You will feel disgusting and at odds with yourself if how you look is not only not how you feel but not how you want the world to see you. This is a lot of nots.

Projecting is drawing attention to the self you want everyone to see. Start at the bottom. Underwear, being as close as it is to the flesh, will remind you all day just who and what you think you are. Jockeys are a good all-purpose knicker if you are at a loss. They say 'healthy'.

Some women choose to make themselves invisible by disguising themselves as the rest of the pack. They might, for instance, wear an Alice band and almost no make-up but an angry red lipstick at night to render themselves indistinguishable from everyone else at a charity bazaar for dogs. But others choose to draw attention to themselves by cultivating a style which is both intriguing, individual and pleasing on the eye.

Be clear what it is you want to project. Cast about for the clothes, face and hair that spells it out. Try to coordinate the look. I'm not saying coordinate clothes, just the look. What's the point in doing a lumberjack top if you put floozy-from-the-circus on the bottom? What will you be saying apart from 'Who am I?'

IDENTITY CRISES

Yes. Who are you? It's a hard one when we all have multiple personalities and it's anyone's guess which will appear on the day. These personalities blend in time to become the same old woman going on about the size of her breasts, but when you are forming the person you will become, which is to say until you are about forty, who wants to put their hand on their heart and say, 'This is me!'

It's not just mood swings. We all have within us the shy person, the enchantress, the mean turd, the perfect hostess, the true friend, the woman of insight and the chilling intellect. It would seem sensible to dress as the dominant personality but only if you wish to be recognised as that person. You may not.

I see no harm at all in confusing the public. If you are feeling desperately shy and low on self-esteem, why not wear something silver and clinging in line with the girl you were last week? This will suggest a shrinking violet trapped in the body of an enchantress which is pretty damn bewitching if you ask me. Who wants to be one-dimensional? Not my daughters.

SOME LOOKS AND HOW TO ACHIEVE THEM

Frail and romantic is best achieved by dresses from
the 1930s or 40s. They look best with clumpy-heeled
open-toed sandals which don't flatter all ankles. A
compromise might have to be made. I'm no style guru
but it's my guess that flip-flops aren't the answer
unless you are doing frail, romantic and just hurt
my foot.

Tough and businesslike will suggest suits to most
people but I think something snappy in riding apparel
could do the trick just as well. It will come from
within. Should you go for riding apparel, under no
circumstances wear stilettos. You will look like a shoe
fetishist. On the other hand, always own one pair of
stilettos. Many occasions call for them and they should
also be worn on many occasions that don't.

Dressing appropriately is advised but there are
only some occasions when inappropriate dressing is
a disaster. To avoid them, it is generally held that to
overdress is better than to underdress but this is quite
wrong.

AN OVERDRESSING MOMENT
FROM MY OWN LIFE

Before I met your father I was asked to a dance by a
boy who went off me almost as soon as he had issued
the invitation. I didn't know. I thought I was still asked
to the dance so I went and had my hair set into a
starling's nest.

When I came home from the hairdressers, I
telephoned him to ask what time he was collecting me.
He was out so I asked his mother. She was at a

loss. When he hadn't contacted me by six, I phoned her again and suggested I go over to their place in a taxi and meet the boy there, which I did, wearing my lilac ball frock with the floral bodice made by my auntie.

The boy was surprised to see me, especially since the dance had a Wild West theme and everyone else was in jeans. I was too brazen to cut my losses and go home. My partner and I spent much of the evening on opposite sides of the room as I overcompensated for the strangeness of my appearance with loud singing and exotic dancing. I never saw him again.

I don't really care what you wear or how you wear it, provided you take into account everything I said about personal safety (see What You Need To Know About Men). Just remember that *feeling* will direct your sense of purpose and so your style. Always approach the mirror with a sense of purpose and a lightness of touch.

ANOTHER MOMENT ILLUSTRATING THE NEED FOR LIGHTNESS OF TOUCH

One night when I was watching one of you in a school play, the woman behind me leant across and said, 'I never knew you wore make-up.'

I said, 'I do sometimes. I am tonight.'

'So I can see,' she bellowed. She advised, in a voice that could be heard in Worthing, that I try a little moisturiser underneath my foundation and blend it well. She roared with laughter when I protested that I had although I hadn't.

Her advice was correct. As to whether she was correct to comment, I refer you to my observations elsewhere on polite conversation.

Watch out for powder as well. Too much is a disaster on the ageing skin where it clings to folds and flying buttresses, but it's even more tragic on a youthful complexion. I never wear any but if you must, put it on and take it off. That way you will be left with glowing, which is all that's required when you are wearing expressions as untrammelled as yours by disappointment.

Use a lip liner to indicate serious intention.

CLEAN

Dirt is a great underminer of a sense of purpose. There is nothing more unfortunate or a bigger giveaway than food stains in obvious places, or worse, in less obvious places. They project sloppy eater and I don't think this works for many people. Before long I will not be available to you to stick stuff in the washing machine, any more than your father will be on hand with the Dreft for delicates, so you should keep an eye on this yourself, starting now.

Don't go out looking dirty. You don't like dirty hair. You should feel just as concerned about dirty clothes. Scuffed shoes you can get away with but only sometimes. Laddered tights were all right in 1995 but now they are finished and to wear them is to invite laughter and scoffing.

This brings me to toenails. Paint them. I don't care with what but anything is better than the foot with five nails wedged solid with soil and other debris. Care for your feet as you would your hands. I haven't and I regret it. Think of the poor girl selling you shoes or waxing your legs. Think of the poor young man who may want to suck your toes. You owe it to them if not yourself. It is only in the matter of cleanliness that you must consider other people. Otherwise, most definitely, please yourself.

PRESERVATION OF SELF

It's never wise to go shopping with a friend. Their judgement is never yours and you can put money on coming home with an item that you will never wear. Or if you do, you will think of them when you wear it and wonder why you are speaking funny.

Equally, be wary of friends who offer to make you clothes. Who knows which personality of yours they imagine is the real you? They will only confuse and upset you. The purchase of clothes and make-up is for you alone. That way you will develop your own taste and display it with confidence and charm. Whatever it is, remember I am your mother and I will always love you.

Rule: Lavender in your drawers makes your clothes smell like lavender. Avoid it until you are ninety-seven.

BEAUTY TIPS

Y ou don't have to be vain to be beautiful but I like
vain. The most interesting women in the world
are vain. I'm thinking of your grandmother. It's from
her that we inherited our preening mirror face with
the half-closed eyes although it's not our best look. It
is from your grandmother that we learn you can wear
the cheapest powder in the supermarket and still keep
your looks.

NUNS

You might meet some interesting nuns who aren't vain.
But what will they have to say about painted toenails
and broken capillaries? I'm not suggesting that beauty
tips should govern a woman's life but a woman without
them in her vocabulary is a poor apology. Nuns, of
course, are brides of Christ. Not a lot of sex there and
sex is definitely an incentive for a proper beauty regime.
   Vanity doesn't have to depend on sexual hope but
even so, it's a rare nun who will describe her skin care
regime which is a shame when it's also a rare nun who

has spots or the telltale signs of premature ageing. I can only put this freak of nature down to very few free radicals in the convent.

By vanity, I mean of course pleasure in your appearance. This is a contradiction in terms when your appearance gives as much heartache as it does delight so I advise a degree of moderation. Spend long hours in front of a mirror looking for defects by all means but know when to stop. Always stop when I'm in the mirror area myself and needing complete peace and quiet.

NATURE'S GIFTS

My own gifts were so singularly lacking that in childhood many people were forced to comment. Auntie Lil said, 'You were a funny-looking little thing. But your mother did her best with fabrics.' And next door's grandmother said, 'Never mind dear, the ugly duckling can turn into a beautiful swan.' Oddly, I remained untouched by these remarks but both these women are now dead. Make of that what you will. I determined to make the most of myself, using not just fabric but anything else I could lay my hands on.

It goes without saying that being born with good bones, thick hair and the muscle tone of a natural athlete helps. But there are many well endowed women who are mistaken for plain because they ignore nature's gifts and you should avoid becoming one of these at all costs. They look wretched. When you are born with gifts as you all have been, nurture them or you will lose them to the mists of time.

Some gifts need less nurturing than others but there are three areas of concern for all women everywhere, gifted or otherwise. Skin, hair and teeth. Pamper your skin, tend to your hair and watch over your teeth and even on your worst days, people will remark on your cleanliness. Cleanliness is a close relation of radiance. And radiant is not a bad thing to be when you are feeling like muck in the gutter.

SKIN – MINE, AN ANECDOTE

When I was eighteen, I went to a beautician, not out of any sense of needing her, more out of curiosity. A beautician was a rare thing in Sydney in those days, like today's shaman, only with more muslin. I expected a little admiration, a lot of patting and possibly a potion or two which would protect my future. She took my face in her hands and I believe she screamed. She looked as if she was screaming.

This woman was a foreigner and knew about skin from Austria or someplace. I used her many years later in a novel about the treachery of beauty. She shook her head in disgust and told me the damage was already done. I had been exposed too often and too long to the sun and very soon lines were going to appear all over my face like the mark of Cain shouting 'Crone! Crone!' at anyone brave enough to meet my eye. This was upsetting so I didn't go back.

My vanity at that time took the shape of many interesting hairpieces, as much eye make-up as I could fit on to a smaller than average lid and tanning. I called it tanning. It was really acquiring a background of sludge for my freckles. I don't remember moisturising though I might have used Ponds as my mother always kept a tub of nourishing cream on the bathroom shelf. Wrinkles would have been forming on my facial dermis like nobody's business.

Learn from me. Start young. Carry a moisturiser with you everywhere and slap it on at every opportunity. Leave off when lumps appear. They indicate overuse.

Since my early thirties I have devoted a fortune to moisturiser, as well as toner, day cream, night cream, neck cream and eye gel though the eye gel usually hardens in the tube from lack of use. I also splash body lotion all over me and sometimes anti-cellulite stuff. How pitiful a battle it is. But how happy I am to wage it. I slop stuff all over me and feel like a rich French adulteress which is a nice way to start and end the day.

YOUR SKIN

Although you all tan divinely, avoid sun on the face. It will give you cancer, lines and eventually piggy eyes. Always cleanse and moisturise. If you are strapped for cash, you may like to try this recipe for a face pack I found in a book. Blend a piece of baker's yeast the size of a walnut with sufficient milk to make a thick cream. Paint evenly all over the face apart from the lips and eyes, spread to one-eighth of an inch thick or less if you have a dry skin, leave on for twenty minutes and wash off with warm water. I don't know what it is supposed to achieve and I've never tried it myself but it sounds . . . cheap.

Even if you neglect your face, moisturise your hands. They will betray you in later life and hand lifts can't be put down to a relaxing holiday or car crash.

THE BLEMISH

I have strong feelings about the squeezing of spots. A girl in my class said her auntie died after squeezing one of hers. Someone said you would only die if the spot was above the nose but even so you can't be too careful. I advocate dabbing a little calamine on the blemish at night and concealer during the day. My mother used to say peroxide but peroxide stinks and the temptation is to pour it into your hair which will ruin it. Calamine will do for day as well as night if you can't afford concealer. Either way you will look as if you have a spot but it will be in recovery.

Above all things, keep your hands away from the affected area. Touching it will only make matters very much worse and soon you will be wearing so much calamine you might as well go out in the baker's yeast.

HAIR

If it's on your head keep it clean and shiny. Elsewhere, only grow it if you wish to make a statement about nature. Be wary about such statements, however. They are acceptable only to like-minded people.

I expect our need to remove all visible body hair has something to do with women pretending to be vulnerable, delicate and unmasculine and that it may be politically unacceptable. Rise above such politics. Get rid of the hair. Shave if you're desperate but not anything resembling a moustache.

For the moustache, or other facial hair should it appear in later life, I recommend electrolysis which is done with a needle. On other body parts there is wax, which can bruise you badly if you attempt it at home, depilatory creams which smell funny, or special laser things. Shaving is cheapest and easiest but you need to be deft with a razor and conscious of stubble. Never shave the bikini area. Bikini stubble is as lovely as fungus.

Should you choose to dye hair at home, regardless of where it is on your body, please use a dark towel as the dye will stain and I know you will not replace what you have ruined.

TEETH

Dental evenness is not necessary for beauty maintenance. I am opposed to too much orthodentistry as it suggests an affinity with the Mormon faith which is linked to polygamy. People with strangely even teeth will usually be bigamists.

Whiteness is different. We have been born with wide smiles and therefore we should make the most of them. Use bicarbonate of soda on a little bit of cotton wool to remove stains but kindly use a bathroom out of earshot when you do so. No one likes the sound of gagging.

Fresh breath is also crucial. See a dentist regularly in case cavities are harbouring antisocial bacteria. If you must have fillings, ask for the white jobs over the mercury ones and if you can't afford them, your father and I will do our best. If our best isn't good enough, get a paper round. Mercury is a contentious area but it is my belief that it lodges in the brain and accounts for much memory loss and falling over.

My own unhappy teeth

Unhappily, when I was a child, it was fashionable among Australian dentists to fill all teeth which were not perfectly formed. As a result I have silver trenches on all four gums which are unsightly and cause me much heartache. Should I end up in a home with mercury on the brain, please apply my lipstick correctly and don't put ribbons in my hair.

Diet

Central to healthy skin, hair and teeth is a good diet. You know as well as I do what that means. The important thing is to eat enough to fill you up and to stop when you are full. There's no point in me telling you what is good for you. It changes from day to day. Watch the papers. Currently wholemeal pasta and rice are in favour along with pulses but I can't abide any of them and they produce more wind than is acceptable in a car.

Remember that a diet without any junk in it is a miserable one. I would be lost without chips. The important thing is not to get fetishy. Some food will make you bloat, some will give you wind, some will give you spots, some indigestion, some stinky breath. None of this matters if you like it. Just don't eat it a lot.

Listen to your body. Some weeks you will be very hungry; some weeks, owing to stress, love or poor health you will find it almost impossible to swallow food. This is usual. If you find yourself very underweight, eat Mars Bars. If you find yourself unacceptably overweight, eat less of everything and take a little more exercise.

On the subject of which weight is acceptable,
know that a woman looks infinitely better with curves
than she does with angles and that a stomach which
protrudes a little is a natural stomach. You may call it
bloating if it makes you feel better. Too fat is only when
you are uncomfortable bending over. You can diet too
much and you can exercise too much and when you
do you will get that look on your face which says I am
miserable, shun me.

NO PAIN WITHOUT GAIN

The following hurt: the shampooing chairs in hair
salons which are enough to make you faint if your neck
is tense from awful hair; eyelash tinting if they get the
stuff in your eyes which too many people do; waxing;
mole removal; cosmetic surgery.

SLEEP

You need it. Get home early. Catching up is not
catching up. It's sleeping in and will make you ill.

ON THE CHEAP

I have told you about the face pack. Looking after your
hair, skin and teeth needn't be expensive even though
I choose to make it so now I am of a certain age.
Vigilance is much more important than extravagance.
But more important than anything is a pleasant and
hopeful expression. You can slap whatever you like on
to your body, but if you are poison within you will be
toxic without and people will notice.

SOME BEAUTY TIPS FOR SPECIAL OCCASIONS

1. Be cautious about having your hair put up at the hairdressers. It only ever looks as if something has fallen on you.

2. To avoid lipstick on your teeth, form your mouth into an O after the last application and insert your index finger, grip it with your lips, then slowly remove it, dragging off any excess.

3. Only smoke if you need the cigarette ash to remove hair tint from the skin.

I don't know any more tips.

Rule: *Beauty is in the eye of the beholder but what would the beholder know? Ask yourself.*

Herbs, potions
and psychic powers

The handiness of psychic powers is grossly underestimated. This is because so few people like to admit they exist. I'm not even sure I think they do although I don't think they don't. I hope they do. I hope we are the psychic family we tell ourselves we are. Certainly we have many telepathic experiences and more often than not, I can guess what you are up to and thinking even though you aren't speaking or even in the same house. I do not actually practise magic or witch-doctoring myself but I like to think I could and I advise you to cultivate your own powers. They are not only helpful in child-raising but you will make many friends if you put it about that you have second sight.

Psychic experience

My first was at school when I was five and had just embarrassed myself by telling everyone I could sing like Elvis Presley. I demonstrated and they said, 'No you can't.' To restore myself in their eyes I boasted that I could make money. They said, 'Go on.' So I blew into the brown paper bag which had contained my packed lunch, popped the bag, opened it, and out fell a sixpence, stunning everyone but mostly me. I knew I had powers after that.

INTUITION

I am prepared to admit that a lot of it is intuition which can be womanly but not necessarily. Your father says he is a transmitter of thoughts but he isn't all that intuitive about other things.

You can and should cultivate your intuition by being endlessly curious about other people's behaviour and putting yourselves into their shoes. Not just in them, in them walking around, getting blisters and taking them off. After a while you get to feel things.

SPELLS

These should be used only with utmost caution. Your auntie in Australia heard of a woman who had fallen out badly with her estranged husband, so stuck his photograph in the fridge and days later he collapsed. Outraged by some politician or other, my sister, a woman given to extravagance, cut his photograph from the paper and shoved it in the freezer. Feeling pleased, she told a colleague who cried, 'Get it out, get it out. Evil that you send out comes back to you threefold.' So your auntie rushed home, unpeeled the photo from the frozen peas and put a hot water bottle on it. The politician lived.

In a similar vein – chain letters

These should be treated as items of evil and returned to the sender in triplicate.

Potions

I'm only average on potions but have gleaned the following over many years as a woman, wife, mother and reader of very old books on household management.

Aches and pains

For toothache: make a very small pellet of cotton wool, soak it in oil of cloves and with the sterilised end of a darning needle, push it into the cavity. I have never tried it but I like the sound of it. If you have no oil of cloves, take paracetamol and go to the dentist.

For vomiting: mix a solution of bicarbonate of soda and glucose and, provided you aren't suffering from poisoning, sip it. You may prefer to keep it in a glass by the bed and look at it which works almost as well. If you need to vomit, as in the time one of you attempted a drug overdose with four paracetamol, drink salt water. You will never attempt a drug overdose again.

To prevent sea sickness, fight nausea and diarrhoea and ease morning sickness drink a cup of ginger tea made with a teaspoon of grated fresh root or dried powder but I would counsel not travelling by sea when you are feeling ill and pregnant.

To cure a cold, rub Vicks on to the soles of your

feet. This makes your grandmother feel better and I thought she invented it, but I met a farmer who also swore by it.

To prevent leg cramp in bed, sleep with corks. This also prevents sleep.

Perspiration can be kept in check with a powdering of bicarbonate of soda in the areas prone to damp.

For nerves, as in exam, boy or job, take sal volatile as recommended by your grandmother or Rescue Remedy as recommended by Bach. When I was going through a very nervous patch owing to trying to be in too many places at once, I was prescribed beta-blockers. I took one and it felt like brain surgery.

All the women in our family are very susceptible to substances. When I took Melatonin, a synthetic hormone which is supposed to reduce jet lag, prevent ageing and re-align the body clock, I had no thoughts for three weeks.

HANDY HINTS WITH POTIONS

For reviving old shoes: mix a tablespoon of milk with 1 dessertspoon of methylated spirits. Use sparingly. On the shoes. Drinking it will not have any noticeable effect on shoes.

To repel cockroaches, soak small cloths in eucalyptus and distribute them around your cupboards.

To get rid of moths from your food cupboard, throw out all your food, clean out the cupboards and every container three times (because moth eggs cleave to tiny cracks) and say a decade of the rosary.

Rule: You can go to jail for using unnatural substances and also round the bend. Even small amounts. Just keep that in mind.

CHARACTER
BUILDING

Handling criticism

Not everyone will like you and not everyone will like everything you do. I don't know how shocking you will find this. Not very, I don't suppose, since you have spent many long years at single sex schools where feelings are made quite plain. But you have been much loved and admired at home, so I wonder. The question is: should you care?

First, are we talking no one at all? Not even anyone? If no one at all likes *you* and it is a matter of personal hygiene, manners or over-assertiveness, then you haven't heard a single thing I've said or read any of the pertinent chapters contained herein. But this is unlikely. You are all careful in your habits and charming in your own way and have many friends to prove it. Should no one at all like something *you have done* – a criminal act, an artistic creation or possibly a rice dish – then you must ask yourself this. Am I pleased with it? If you are pleased with it, then that is enough.

It is, I should warn you, very hard to continue liking something you have done when no one else at all likes it. This stems from why you did it in the first place. I don't think I would be stretching a point if I said more likely than not so someone would like it. I would be inclined to seek advice if you or your act is universally despised and you don't know why or you don't care.

If only one or twenty people don't like you or something you have done, but just as many, including yourself, do, then you can be pleased with yourself. It marks you and your act as controversial. To be controversial is to be talked about; to be talked about is to be making your mark. A mark, however small, is a good thing to make.

WHAT I DO IF SOMEONE DOESN'T LIKE ME

I feel terrible. I say, 'Who cares?' but I am just being brave. I feel terrible. I work out how I can save the situation. I toss, I turn, I talk to everyone about it. I accost strangers. I tell them what has happened. I phone your father at work. He tries to counsel me. I don't listen to him. He tries to soothe me. I tell him he's talking through his hat. He tells me he's in a meeting. I phone my sister, my mother, I talk, I rail. I say yes, yes, of course you're right, but I'm not really listening. Then I decide what I want to do. Very often it is to say, 'Who cares?' and mean it. Possibly I will plan a little light revenge.

SELF-ESTEEM

We didn't have self-esteem when I was growing up. We had too big for her boots, thinks herself smart and inferiority complex. They were, I suppose, part and parcel of the same thing but there is something a little bit oozy about self-esteem which I can't quite take to. I would rather talk in terms of confidence. Having too much, too little, or just enough.

You need just enough confidence to shrug off criticism and twice as much again to accept it when it's helpful. You or your act aren't necessarily reduced by input from someone else. That's what they say. I still find this very difficult to accept.

In my experience, sensitive people are harder on themselves than anyone else and if you learn a little about self-editing and self-evaluation, which you will in time, you can afford to tell other people to get stuffed when they think they know better. You won't of course. You will be far too well-mannered. But you can think it with impunity.

A HELPFUL PERSPECTIVE

In the field of artistic endeavour, it is impossible to please everyone. You must accept this before you embark on it. But business being business, you will get more work the more people you please. What you have to decide is how much of a compromise you are prepared to make. My advice is to be prepared to make endless compromises – there are a thousand ways to skin a rabbit (see earlier) – but suggest the compromises yourself. Don't have them forced upon you. Other people talk such crap.

Rule: Only show me your writing if you want an honest opinion. Then give me a break and don't sulk about it.

WHEN TO LIE AND STEAL

Your grandmother used to say, 'The truth always hurts,' which was the best argument I ever heard for lying. But mostly, I'm against it. It's just wet. You should own up even if it's just to prove you're big enough to take responsibility for your own mistakes. Everyone likes a brave person. Everyone likes a brave and honest person, especially if they are pretty, have nice smiles and clean hair. Honesty and a clear conscience are the keys to mental health. You can go too far in this regard, however.

WHAT AN IDIOT

When I was eight or nine and a bit of a geek, someone whistled in the classroom when the teacher was Sister Jude. It was madness. Sister Jude was a psychopath who threw blackboard dusters. She demanded to know who had done it. It wasn't me. I don't know who it was. No one owned up and the silence was dreadful. Then what a lark! What a jape! I whistled. Sister Jude went icy. We all went icy. She whispered that whoever had done it had better own up or there would be trouble for everyone. I owned up. I said, 'I didn't do it the first time though.' But where was the proof? No one believed me except the person who had whistled the first time and she must have been laughing her head off. I was punished. I don't know how. It is too terrible for me to remember.

BUT I FELT BETTER FOR IT

This was the truth hurting though not very much. Maybe I shouldn't have owned up. Maybe I shouldn't have whistled. But the whistle gave me a lot of pleasure and I would have felt like a weasel if I hadn't admitted to it. Call this a Catholic conscience but I'd rather have a Catholic conscience than no moral fibre.

YOU WANT TO BE LIKED, DON'T YOU?

People admire you if you have moral fibre and who likes a weasel? OK, who would want to be in the trenches with a weasel, or halfway up a mountain on the end of a short rope? Who would trust a weasel with their life? There are times when you should lie (see Sensible Lying below) but by and large, the honourable path is the better one. If you're caught out in a lie you look like pus. Everyone remembers. They will say, 'She's such a little liar.' It mightn't hold you back in business or politics, or preclude friendships with royal personages, but your reputation will be besmirched in certain circles for ever. What's more, it can become a habit and habitual liars go mad in the end from living in a tissue of deceit.

INSANITY

Worse than lying to others is lying to yourself. This is destructive, foolhardy and very bad for long-term prospects. Here are some examples of lying to yourself: he loves me; everyone loves me; I can do this on my ear; I am very ill; I'll get up at six; it wasn't my fault; no one will notice; everyone's looking; I am brilliant; I am hopeless; everything's fine; everything's hopeless; this can wait until tomorrow; I have to do this now; I am tall. I could go on.

Some self-delusion is harmless conceit. What's it matter if you tell yourself you look like Isabella Rosselini or Frank Bruno when you're short, plump and pink? What matters is when you know in your bones that everything isn't as it should be. Then you must confront your demons. You must turn, you must face them, you must look them squarely in the eye. Then you must tell them they are chicken feed.

DEMONS

The following crop up regularly: fear of failure; fear of success; fear of loneliness; fear of people; fear of food; fear of starving; fear of ugliness. Get the picture? Fear. To overcome fear you must confront it but you can confront nothing if you lie a lot.

Deception will be second nature to you. So used will you be to fabricating a pleasant and glossy alternative that acknowledging any terrible truth will be out of the question. You will know the demon is there but you will stay in hiding. Calamity will await you – not hell now we no longer have it, but something hellish. Possibly

jail, a dreadful hangover or feeling very ill all of
the time. (More on Demons later.)

SLOPPY THINKING

I don't like stealing either. Call me old-fashioned. If
you inadvertently take something from a shop without
paying for it, you should pay for it next time. The
people in the shop will like you and possibly give you
something free. Possibly not. Getting away with it isn't
the point. Shoplifting stinks.

It's currently the go to adopt a free and easy attitude
to taking what isn't yours but it's rubbish, isn't it?
If you can justify nicking a plastic bauble, you can
justify nicking a diamond ring. The only difference is
the long stretch you might get for the ring. There's no
moral difference. It's the taking without paying that
counts. You don't steal from shops or anyone else,
however much you despise them, because to take what
isn't rightfully yours subverts order. Having said that,
if you were starving and I truly had no other means
whatsoever of feeding you, I'd nick what I could where
I could and hope to heaven no one asked your father
about it.

HOPELESS LIARS – YOUR FATHER

There's absolutely no point in even attempting to lie if
your face gives you away or your every tricky thought
is betrayed by your unconscious. Look at your father.
He tells a lie, his mouth goes funny and his nostrils
dilate. He has an awkward thought and splat, out
it flops.

Once we invited a woman called Tessa to supper. She had enormous breasts which your father admired hugely. He had been going on about them for hours before she arrived then, when he opened the door, he cried, 'Bresta, how lovely to see you.' You don't even think about serious lying if you have his sort of handicap. Otherwise there are certainly times when you should.

SENSIBLE LYING

Obviously you lie when to tell the truth will cause disproportionate pain. Who needs to be told they are ugly? Who needs to be told you forgot them? Who wants to hear their husband or wife has committed adultery? Not me. If your father has a mistress, he owes it to me never to let it cause me a minute's grief and to make it up to me with jewels, gifts and extra attention. The last thing he should do is unburden himself just so's I can be burdened with it. I will know if he has a mistress just by looking at him but I will only ask him about it if I want a divorce.

EXAGGERATION AND EMBELLISHMENT

This isn't lying. I do it all the time and would be lost without it.

HOME TRUTHS

This is what your grandmother meant when she said truth hurts. She meant truth as in 'You are a lying little schemer and you will come to no good. You haven't tidied your room and you haven't found the toothpaste.' I don't really care for them myself though I think it's OK to tell your father he is fat because I fear he will have a heart attack and die before we get to live in the south of France.

Rule: Only tell someone they look gorgeous if they really sort of do. They will know they don't and never trust you again. I learnt that from you after I sent one of you off to the school dance in the wrong clothes, said you'd never looked better and then got the photos back.

DEMONS AND HOW
TO SLAY THEM

M aybe you should know more about spotting
demons and confronting them. The demon is
a rational or irrational fear that you are refusing to
recognise although I will have been trying to tell you.
You will feel ill, sweaty, be getting unusual cramps and
flickering sensations, tossing and turning at night and
having terrible dreams. What can it be? Lyme disease?
You might put on weight, lose weight, feel weepy, bad
tempered and permanently dissatisfied. Doctors will be
mystified. Your family will be perplexed and prone to
yawning in your company.

'She's right,' you must say at this juncture to
yourself. 'There is a demon that I must confront.' It
might be something you have committed yourself to
that you can't face; it might be some*one* you have
committed yourself to you can't face; it might be a
course of action you have embarked upon you know
is wrong; but much more likely it will be a behaviour
pattern you have embraced that is self-destructive.

You could be phobic. You could be pregnant. I'm

not talking about grudges. Grudges are different. You can nurse a grudge for as long as you like and imagine it gives you pleasure though it will only be burning up life units.

A DEMON I ONCE HAD

When I was extremely small I was obsessed by murderers and used to think I could hear footsteps outside my window in the dead of night. I would imagine they were heading towards the back door and then I would hear someone trying the handle. I'd lie awake straining but never be sure. Then one night, I was sure. Definitely footsteps. The murderer had come.

I threw myself out of bed and wriggled on my stomach through the house until I reached my parents' room. My father was in hospital so I woke my mother who, even then, was small. I told her there was someone outside and she jumped out of bed, crying 'Stand back,' to me and 'Who's there?' to the door. God she was brave. 'It's me,' someone called and indeed it was. A relative of my father's, a little disorientated after a night out but absolutely positive that he was himself. My mother ordered a taxi and despatched the demon in a flash. I can't remember if I stopped hearing footsteps after that but let's say I did for the sake of the argument.

HOW TO BANISH THEM

You can a) get help from a professional or b) decide to help yourself. I would suggest course b) first, since it is less expensive and less time-consuming and I hate it when professionals ask you about your relationship with your mother.

Courage

This is how you help yourself. First work out what's bothering you. How easy this is will depend on your honesty which is why you mustn't get into shoplifting or other shady habits. You will have a clue. Certain thoughts will drive you crazy. You must pursue those thoughts to their source. The source will have horns and cloven hooves.

A demon is created by failure to accept (see Keeping Your Feet On The Ground earlier). It will be something that requires a different course of action from the one you are taking and you will need to answer a lot of hard questions honestly. An example might be banging your head against a brick man. Let's look at that one.

An example – the brick man

He will be an unrequited love (see Losers later). Here your way forward is simple. You must forget him. You will say I can't, I love him. I'm telling you, you can. Reinvent yourself as a woman who doesn't need a jerk like that in her life. Reinvent him as the last person you want hanging about and substitute him with another interest. Why are you fixating anyway? Scared of finding Mr Right? If you want to stay single and celibate, stay single and celibate. No one will care.

An example without a love interest

Say you can't keep a job. I will want to know why you can't keep a job but say I'm out of the country so you haven't had me going on and on about it in a fruitless and upsetting way. What's going on here, you will want to know. Why is your mother out of the country?

Maybe I have a record deal in Nashville and you have gone from one job to the next, growing more and more fretful about your failure to stick. You will be thinking you are a failure, that you have antisocial tendencies, that your education was a waste of time and that if anyone has a record deal it should be you. But hang on. That's what I would say if I was there.

You are a sensible, intelligent and worthwhile person so whatever is going on is unnatural. You must take a look at the jobs you have tried and write down why you went for them and whether you had any reservations to begin with. What were the reservations? If there were alarm bells, why did you ignore them? Describe how you felt while you were doing the job. Contented? Fulfilled? Insulted? Ask yourself why you left. Were you fired? Did you stomp out? Did you slink out? The answers to all these questions will provide pointers. Oh yes they will. If you can't see them, phone me at the studio.

Now you will have a rough idea of the problem. Either you are going for the wrong sort of job, or you are going for the right sort of job and behaving like a crazy person once there. Let's say you are going for the wrong sort of job. Why? Are you trying to please someone apart from yourself? Are you terrified of looking unglamorous, unsuccessful, unpopular and underachieving when everyone expects you to be a juggler? Or do you want to be a juggler, no one thinks you are up to it, so you are going after the wrong sort of job and failing at it to make a point?

Let's say you're going for the right sort of job but failing at it. Could we have fear of commitment here? Or fear of a routine? Or resentment of structure? These are the kinds of questions you must ask yourself and answer truthfully. After that you must cure yourself.

CURE

Once you've recognised the problem causing your funny behaviour pattern by answering the questions you have posed for yourself, you just change the pattern.

Sometimes the problem recurs – the brick man for instance. You might acknowledge that the man you thought was the stuff of dreams is actually a bloody nightmare and get shot of him only to replace him with his doppelgänger.

If you find yourself so ensnared, you have to be very, very brave. You must wean yourself off the type for ever. Maybe it helps to know why you're drawn to them, maybe not. Sometimes agonising over the root of a problem is unhelpful and distracting. Move on. That's my advice. Say, 'Demon, begone' and move on, as slowly and carefully as you like, to become a new, stronger, less fearful you with none of the symptoms of Lyme disease.

If none of the above works, get help but leave me out of it.

Rule: *Lack of fearfulness is almost as bad. There's nothing wrong with a little fear. It keeps your wits sharp and your bowels working.*

SELF
SUFFICIENCY

INDEPENDENCE

Does independence mean leaving home? No. As your mother, I can assure you it's perfectly possible to live with me for ever and still be a mature, self-sufficient and responsible adult, sound in mind and body. You can stay home as long as you like, provided you obey the house rules.

This could be a sticking point because the house rules that suit the average very tired parent whose house it is aren't necessarily those that suit the average twenty-year-old daughter whose life is chiefly night. If this happens you soon know, as we have already, on occasion, discovered.

HOUSE RULES

My requirements are modest: pitching in and letting me know what you're up to. Letting me know can be a sore point because I can see it isn't easy to break away from a romantic moment to say, 'I must ring my mother.' However you must ring your mother if it is after two in the morning and you are going to be much later or I will be lying awake listening for your key in the lock and seeing your body in a dark alley.

I will possibly wake your father and he will be very irritated and say to you next morning and for many days afterwards, 'Why do you worry your mother? A phone call. That's all it takes.'

LEARNING CURVE

Of course it is pleasant to be answerable to no one. I have never been in that happy position but I'm sure it is. Conversely, it could be terrible having no one to care. When you leave home, you get six of one and half a dozen of the other. But it's my belief that everyone should leave their parents' home sooner or later just to see what it's like. You can go away, come back, go away, come back, returning each time with a larger and fresher understanding of what a joy it is to be home. Or not. This is a pleasant pattern and cushions a blow I might otherwise feel too painfully.

One day you will meet someone and want to set up your own permanent home or you may not meet someone but decide you would like a place of your own, on your own. I will be able to live with that, provided you phone every day, visit once a week and come home when you're sick. You must leave when the time is right and this can be any age from eighteen to forty.

TIMING – EXAMPLE ONE

Your grandmother used to say to us, 'If you don't like it, leave.' She was a great believer in the young leaving the nest to stand on their own two feet a.s.a.p. and we all did. But everything's so much more expensive these days. You have to be extremely flush to be self-supporting. And family life is so much more fun. I think so.

Your grandmother is a good example of someone leaving because hers wasn't. She took off at fifteen and who can blame her? She was one of twelve children, home was a sheep station in the middle of nowhere, she'd had enough of school and she wanted the excitement of town life. Her father let her go on condition that she move into a boarding house supervised by a respectable Catholic woman. There she crept out of the window at night to go to wild parties given by the gay man who worked in the haberdashers. Eventually she moved from the town to the city with her friend Flo and they shared many happy flats until they both married in their early thirties. I love her story but don't even think of trying it for yourself.

I don't know any respectable Catholic women with boarding houses and even if I did, I couldn't handle worrying about her window. In my view, fifteen is far too young though I have no objection to eighteen, provided I, or another close relative, can reach you by car in less than fifteen minutes. You could, of course, go away to university at eighteen, but none of you has shown the slightest inclination to do that and all have said you want to continue your education near home in London which I think is very wise.

PREPARATION

You might think I haven't prepared you adequately
for independence by being too controlling, nosey and
insistent on having you about the place. Perhaps you
would have enjoyed boarding school. I don't think so.
You have all hated school trips and only went because
I made you. I only made you so you wouldn't look
dysfunctional.

I've never believed independence had anything to
do with being sent away from home in infancy. No.
For me, independence springs from a growing sense
of responsibility as well as desperation at unnatural
confinement.

Growing up is the best preparation for leaving home.
Growing up, growing fed up, growing fed up with your
parents and the view your parents have of you as a
child. This can be overwhelming and not something I
would necessarily notice owing to me thinking we all
get along so jolly well.

SISTERS

Although I can't see it in our house, brothers and sisters
can make family life just as claustrophobic, especially
so for older sisters, I gather. Both your auntie and your
grandmother suffered terribly, or so they say. Your
grandmother says she was permanently scarred by
having to take responsibility for a wayward younger
sister who hated school as much as I did and would
flee from the classroom in a rage to take refuge in a
tall tree.

'Get her sister,' the nuns would say and your
grandmother would be summoned to stand at the

trunk and talk her sister down. The sister wouldn't be talked. She would climb further up the tree and call the nuns every swear word she could think of as they glared at your grandmother. It was a nightmare and your grandmother never forgave the sister. This was the sister who was famous for writing brilliantly funny letters and making things up. I am supposed to be like her although not on account of the brilliantly funny letters. Once I left home, no one ever accused me of making stuff up.

Leaving home is an outgrowing affair but it doesn't have to happen if the home is a laugh, accommodating and well-heated.

TIMING – EXAMPLE TWO

I couldn't wait to leave home myself. I wanted to leave home, leave town, and leave the country and I was able to do it all by marrying a foreigner young. You are not to attempt this either. It only worked for me because the foreigner was your father.

It wasn't that I didn't love my family. I did. But life at home wasn't very relaxed in those days and there wasn't much leeway for the child to turn into an adult and occupy the same bedroom comfortably. I left home three months after my nineteenth birthday, on the day I was married, and I have no regrets about that whatsoever. Who knows what would have happened if I hadn't? I was getting pretty desperate.

WHAT YOU NEED TO LEAVE

As well as a sense of urgency, you need the wherewithal to survive independently when you leave. This means not just enough money to pay the rent, but enough to pay for food, fares, phone, gas and electricity bills, groceries, clothes, dry-cleaning, haircuts and outings. This is a huge outlay so you have to look at your means very carefully.

Sometimes the need to get out is greater than the means available which is why girls go on the game or turn to lives of crime. Please let me know if this state of affairs occurs and your father and I will talk to you sensibly about redecorating your room, buying in different food and getting a mobile phone which can send special late home signals.

INDEPENDENCE OF THOUGHT

I don't need to go on about this because all of you have it and have had from the cradle.

FINAL THOUGHT

Don't leave home in anger. Always negotiate. I won't mind lugging the suitcases or even driving you to the airport, provided you know the door will always be open if you want to come back.

Rule: If you can't keep your room tidy, at least keep your door closed.

MONEY

Having grown up without any, I have only modest respect for money and this, as you will be aware, has given your father heart failure on many occasions, as well as hay fever. Since I'm not in any position to say for a fact that I'm right and he's wrong, I'll confine myself to a few brief points on fiscal matters which will inform if not impress you.

YOUR ALLOWANCE

Since you were thirteen, we have given you a monthly allowance from which you were supposed to meet your clothing, present and outings expenses. The idea was to teach you the value of money. This failed. You all have had to be subsidised. But you have all had the grace to realise that holiday jobs were part of the answer so you must have learnt something.

SICK FEELING

Your attitude to money is completely dependent on what you can live with, never mind on. A permanent gnawing feeling in the pit of your stomach and a reluctance to open bank statements is a clue that all is not well. You will have spent more than you are earning, or we are giving you, and you will be wondering how you can possibly repay your debts.

Your father and I will help you out whenever we can but since our position ranges so widely from feast to famine, you won't be able to rely on us. Our famines are always a little heart-stopping but no matter how reckless I am, I have always listened to my stomach.

MONITOR REGULARLY

Don't be a wimp about it. Always know how much you owe and what you are owed. Comb the back of your mind for assets and possible sources of income and check them out, bearing in mind there is no money in the family other than ours that you can expect to inherit. Don't even try to kid yourself. Your stomach won't be fooled. It will only go from gnawing to taking bites out of itself.

Begin with a total of what is or isn't in the bank. I check it by telephone using my special 'you might think this is a problem but it doesn't worry me' voice. Write the amount at the top of a page, draw a line down the centre of the page and on one side total up what you are owed and on the other side further outgoings which have yet to appear on the statement. Remember all standing orders and any payments made by debit card of which you have no real record having thrown away the slips. For accuracy, overestimate the cost of restaurant meals and what you have spent on taxis, clothes and haircuts. It's impossible, believe me.

You will notice that what you are owed is a very small column while the other is a long one. This is normal. To still your racing heart, do the sums in your head. Do not use a calculator. You will soon become so good at mental arithmetic that being in debt will become a positive thing.

If you are in serious debt with no hope of paying it back given your income and current outgoings, you must cut right back on the outgoings. If you are of school age, forget outings. If you have left school and home, either move back home or stop going out, walk to work and take a second job. Just do it. It is disastrous for your mental health to build a debt you cannot repay.

Owing to extremely long custom and massive amounts going in and out, we have a bank which is helpful and mostly sympathetic. But never tell yourself that the bank is there to help. The bank is only there to help itself to your money which is why they like you to be in debt. They like you to have as big a debt to them as possible, to have it for as long as possible and to have a regular income which keeps those interest repayments coming in, month in, month out.

On the other hand, you do need to have a reasonable relationship with them.

LOVE THE BANK

Never be frightened of the bank manager. Get to know him or her. You won't get to be that friendly because banks move their managers every three or four weeks these days in case they form an attachment to their customers and let them have money cheap. Your father has always been a great one for keeping the bank in the picture. He rings the manager of the day and explains where the money is coming from to repay the overdraft and they are always grateful. So am I.

Even so

When we were living in Australia and didn't have the sentimental attachment we have to our bank here, I shopped about. I was constantly remortgaging and getting better deals and in the end I began to think of myself as a monetary giant. By the time we returned to England, I was ready to ditch sentiment and take on the entire City, so I decided to convert our mortgage to a repayment one. I went to our bank because they knew us and the bank sent a rep to the house.

I asked him in passing where the balance went on a repayment mortgage after the interest had been taken out of the monthly repayment. I said, 'Surely it reduces the capital.' He said, 'Ah . . . maybe not.' I said, 'Surely. Where else could it go?' He wasn't sure. He asked for a Panadol. I said I was amazed he wasn't sure when he was from the bank. I said I wasn't a banker myself but it was plain to me, unless of course something fishy and fraudulent was going on.

He said he would have to refer to his branch. His branch said it would have to refer to head office and many days later, I was assured in writing that the balance did indeed reduce the capital.

How impressive is that? I was pretty impressed. Familiarise yourself with banking terms so no one can pull the wool over your eyes. (See How To Buy A House.)

SMALL PRINT

When you are committing money to anything, always read the small print of every document and if you don't understand it show it to me. You will be surprised at how often the people who send it to you don't know what it means either.

NIGGARDLINESS

Don't be rash but don't stint yourself. There's nothing worse than a miser or hoarder. If you are not impoverished, spend. You won't ever get to have that day again and if that was the day you should have had a bottle of champagne, what a tragedy not to have had it. Take the holiday, have the party, give the gift.

Splashing out is my favourite thing though I have no great interest in acquiring stuff. Stuff is an encumbrance and my dislike of it could well stem from my need to be on the move as often as possible. It's my belief that you *need* very few things. Some will acquire sentimental value but even then, better to treasure the memory of an occasion or person in my opinion. You need money for shelter, food, and clothes and everything after that is a bonus. But that's my opinion only. Spend however you like as I know you already do.

FT-SE AND DOW

Can't help you. Sorry.

PENSION SCHEMES AND OTHER INSURANCES

They cost your father and me a fortune and are mainly to protect you from burdens you don't need, like us when we are aged, infirm or dead. You are too young to have to consider any for yourself but I advise you to look into them when you become property owners.

ACQUIRING IT

We may leave you money in our will. Then again, we may not. The one thing you can be sure about with money is that you can never be sure you will always have it. It comes. It goes. In our family it has come by hard work. Perhaps you will find careers that pay spectacularly well. Maybe you won't. Hardly anyone does. But it makes sense to take into account your tastes and needs when pursuing a career because you will be miserable if poverty is unacceptable to you and you become a nun. You could marry well. You could win the Lottery. You could make a lucky investment. You're on your own with all these schemes. What's mine is yours, however, until I drop.

Rule: Buying endless clothes from charity shops could turn out to be an investment but probably not. Cull. Your rooms can't take much more.

Health

Many people have asked me of our family, 'Are you a pack of hypochondriacs or what?' I say, 'Are you talking to me, fatso?' There's nothing wrong with hypochondria. It's a right and proper interest in staying alive. Never be frightened of strong language when you are defending an important position.

Everyone knows that without early diagnosis we only have ourselves to blame should we die. And it stands to reason you can only make an early diagnosis if you watch your body like a hawk for significant changes. Hypochondria is no more than eternal vigilance. Only a fool eschews it and not for a minute are you fools. The important thing is not to become a bore.

What is a health bore

A health bore is someone who thinks his own health is far more interesting than yours. Show a modicum of concern for the friend who says, 'Me too.' It doesn't have to be much.

EXAMPLES OF VIGILANCE

At approximately your age, I discovered a hitherto
unnoticed bone in my ankle. I went to the doctor and I
said, 'I had polio in this leg and now I have a new bone
in my ankle.' He said, 'I have people to attend to who
are dying.'

When I was twenty years older, I found a brown
mark on my arm and I demanded a referral to the
hospital. The hospital said, 'We call these marks
liver spots but we will cut this one out if you insist.' I
insisted.

Listen, a bone can mean anything and so can a
brown mark.

SICKOS – YOUR FATHER

Your father, you will have noticed, takes up a lot of
space in the medicine cabinet. He has many unfortunate
afflictions. Sneezing, skin problems, bad back, snoring,
other breathing difficulties and digestive problems
from the top of his tract to his very bottom. These all
make him unhappy but he is not prepared to tackle the
problem at source. If he ate less of what was good for
him and none of the other rubbish and went to the gym
more than once a month, his health would look up.
Don't waste your breath on people with afflictions who
aren't prepared to help themselves. They will drain you
of crucial resources.

A SIDE ISSUE

This applies especially to men. Bear in mind that when
you marry, you promise to stick it out in sickness and
in health so to attach yourself to a man with a poor
constitution is asking for trouble. Try to anticipate,
although it isn't easy. Your grandmother married a
rugby player who lost his spleen in a car accident – it
must have just rolled away – and was never the same
again. Added to that, he liked a drink, so for many
years went into hospital on an annual basis with ulcers
and ultimately no pancreas or gall bladder. The visiting
she put in! She was a martyr to it.

YOUR OWN RESPONSIBILITY

Look after your health and you will be doing your
next of kin a massive favour. I'm not going to say that
you are all more or less healthy because every mother
knows the minute she opens her mouth, one of her
children will go down with typhus. You have inherited
a tendency to allergies from your father but thankfully
you have them under control. The correct way to stay
healthy is get enough exercise, sleep, fibre, vitamins
and medical attention. Never be frightened of going to
the doctor if you sense all is not well with you. It is why
we have evening surgery.

IN THE MIND

You will come across people who claim they have
never had a day's illness in their lives. Don't expect
to like them. They have pink cheeks, loud laughs and

bad teeth because they don't go to the dentist either. It's only a man who is numb of skull who can ignore the message from his body that his heart is sore. I'm speaking of course of the psychosomatic illness.

It's nothing to be ashamed of. You may very well have symptoms with no organic root but something will be wrong. Possibly your life. Your psychosomatic illness will be alerting you to the fact. Tingling in the face? You will be unhappy in love. But it could be creeping paralysis so get it checked.

A FRIGHTENING SYMPTOM NO ONE TOOK SERIOUSLY AFTER YOUR FATHER PROPOSED TO ME.

I was only seventeen when your father first proposed and I believe I found the whole thing so upsetting I went into shock. I kept pretending to faint. I'd walk along the road, whoops, down I'd go. I'd wait there for a bit and people would step over me. What does that say about the human race when I wasn't reeking of methylated spirits and looked clean?

Usually I only dropped when your father was there and after a while he just stepped over me too, so fairly soon I stopped doing it. I was in denial. When you are in denial it is perfectly OK to behave oddly. If I was similarly placed again, I think I would tell people I was in denial and then they would be more sympathetic.

Imagining your hair is falling out, suspecting you are losing your sight and that your ovaries are exploding are all terrible symptoms and if you tell me about them I will be very nice to you. Provided you don't go on and on.

How do you know you are sick?

You will know when you are truly sick because you won't want to watch television, eat or read. You will only be able to lie in bed with your eyes closed and even though you will have many pressing things to do, and some of these will be enjoyable, you won't be able to attempt them.

The odd pain here and there doesn't mean you are sick but it should be monitored. Ditto the occasional sore throat, runny nose, headache and back pain or odd spot or lump. I don't know about the weird burning sensation you sometimes get on a point in your leg. It could be an early symptom of spontaneous combustion for which there is no known cure. Prevention is to avoid wearing unnatural fibres.

How do you know when someone else is sick?

A sick person is usually green. Sometimes there is blood oozing from the nose, mouth or ear. There may be a high fever, vomiting or coma. Coma is different from heavy sleep because no amount of yodelling directly into the ear will cause a reaction. When you are absolutely certain that someone else is sick, you should offer sympathy or dial 999. Threatening to dial 999 is sometimes an excellent determinant of just how profound the sickness is.

None of this counts if it is your child who is sick. Then you must do everything possible, starting with bed rest, kindness and special food. Unless of course you think they are skiving and you need to be somewhere. Then you send them to school.

When you need to go to hospital

Occasionally I haven't taken you to hospital when I should have, but more often than not, I have taken you to hospital when I needn't have. You have all been a little accident prone and broken limbs on several occasions. The main symptom of a broken limb will be bone sticking out through the skin. Otherwise there will be crookedness in the limb, swelling and a tendency on the part of the injured person to sleep and whimper. Screaming is usually hysteria.

You should always go to hospital if you have fallen from a tree or been knocked down by a car or feel your kidneys are failing. Ditto heart and lungs.

When someone else needs to go to hospital

It is wise to take all children to hospital who have had bad falls and are showing any of the above symptoms of a broken limb. You won't want to after the first few occasions because you soon discover that waiting in Casualty is like waiting for a train during a transport strike with a whole bunch of people on a day outing for the criminally insane. You will be tempted to say, 'Let's see how it is in the morning.'

You ought not to do that with cuts which might need stitching. Effective stitching has to be done promptly according to my hairdresser whose husband put his hand through a plate glass window and dripped blood all over her new carpets for six hours. One of his fingers has gone all funny, owing to leaving it too late. In the event of heads being stuck in things, there is the fire brigade as a sensible alternative.

Should you come across a sick friend demanding to go to the hospital, always be prepared to drive them there but don't promise to wait. You may find yourself still in Casualty several days later because children are seen first.

THE GYM

I am pleased to see that you are all energetic and like to take exercise but a word about the gym. A man I know burst a blood vessel in his head doing the bench press and your father gets asthma just breathing when he is there. Walking is good.

That's enough on health. It doesn't take too long to get boring. Eat your greens.

Rule: Your heart beating is a good sign. Listening to it obsessively in case it skips or falters or pounds is just a phase.

How to be Successful

KNOWING WHAT YOU WANT
AND HOW TO GET IT

To get on in the world you must a) know what you want and b) decide how you are going to get it. This is the simple rule of focus. I say simple but here's a crazy thing. Focus now has such a bad name that the only people who admit to having it *are* crazy. They have eyes bulging out of their heads like rabid politicians and they spit when they speak. I spit. I have focus.

The average person has just about given up on it, not wanting to be pinned down. There's a generalised hope that fate will shuffle them into position and that what is meant to be is what is meant to be. This hocus-pocus is no substitute for focus. Only settle for that fate stuff when everything else has let you down or you have had a lobotomy. Then you may call it accepting. Otherwise call your own shots.

The world may be in the grip of an indecision crisis but I counsel you above all things to have no part of it. Get bulgy eyes and spit if you must, but get focus. It will help if you have passion first. Where has passion gone? I ask as a mother as well as a woman of some passion herself. Did it vanish with the rise of pocket money and TVs in the bedroom?

If you look into your soul and find none, you might have to settle for compromise. Follow your heart's desire, but if your heart doesn't desire anything much, consult your head which will consider your options in a detached and, with any luck, fruitful manner. There are many people who prefer the head route over the heart. I like the heart/head route myself. It's the one I have always tried to take and one day I know I will write a song about it with clever tambourine accompaniment.

A PASSION – MINE

My passion was for writing. I knew from the time I was four that that was what I wanted to do. There was a brief moment when I was drawn to the life of a droving hillbilly singer but I let it pass and I've never regretted it. With time, it became apparent that I had made a wise choice; not only did nothing else attract me, I couldn't do anything else.

I considered my options. I said you can't just be a writer, you must write to make money and support yourself so I joined a newspaper while I thought about novels. Eventually I realised novels don't just pop out of your head; you must practise on something else, so I did two factual books.

Knowing I could now manage more than two thousand words on the same subject, I wrote the untitled novel mentioned earlier. This failed, I struggled, then I wrote a couple of comic novels under the assumed name of a column I was doing for a woman's magazine. They were published and now I can proudly say I am one of London's top ten thousand novelists. Not bad for a little girl from the Sydney suburbs.

I was lucky I had the passion to go after what I wanted with gusto. It meant I could plot a path. My passion took me further down that path. It not only took me down it, it sustained me in the many bleak moments I encountered along it.

More about me – my suffering

I began as a copy girl. In Australian newspapers in those days, you didn't get much lower forms of life than the copy girl, but you had to be one until some senior journalist died and everyone moved up a grade. A senior journalist died, a junior journalist became a senior journalist, a cadet journalist became a junior journalist and a copy boy or girl got a cadetship. For me, no one died.

One day, after eighteen months, I was sent to buy juice for a subeditor who decided when I handed him a tin that he wanted it in a carton. He tossed the tin at me and said to go back for a carton; I threw the tin back at him and told him to get it himself and then I had to resign as a point of honour. Things looked bleak. But it never occurred to me to try something else. For me, there was nothing else.

What you can learn from this

If you haven't been born with a passion, as I was, you can cultivate one. Look at your interest in music and art history and literature. I see passion burgeoning in all of you. When it comes to launching a career, what matters isn't so much what you want as what's available on the day and whether you can stand the dirt, the grime and the poor pay longer than anyone else at the bottom of the ladder.

It doesn't matter whether you are guided by your heart or your head, be prepared to start at the bottom and to endure months and possibly years of humiliation and learning. Make yourself learn by asking questions. It's no big deal. We all did it. The bottom was the usual place for my generation to start and I'm a little hurt that your generation expects otherwise. What do you think? You're better than we were?

Of course you are better educated and very well informed and this will count for something. But mark my words, it's a mistake to turn your nose up at the bottom when it is a means to an end. It's the end that should be within your focus. The end should sustain you.

WHEN YOUR HEART'S DESIRE
LETS YOU DOWN

Sometimes your heart's desire can let you down. Though you pursue it with a mind ever so single, you fail. Especially in the area of invention, both scientific and creative. Possibly your time isn't right or maybe you got your product wrong. It happens.

Your choice is to keep trying, to plug away, or to cut your losses. It's a personal one. But time is an important factor and so is money. Sooner or later, plugging away fruitlessly will be a waste of it. Maybe walk away and come back later. Maybe get something else going at the same time. Take advice. I will always be there to offer it.

IF AN INTEREST NOT A PASSION LETS YOU DOWN

Don't be afraid to change horses mid-stream. What works for one period of your life may not work for another. Keep your options open by staying curious, fit and socially acceptable. A passion may emerge in good time. Keep an eye out for it but never approach strangers in the street in your quest to find one. It's not that urgent.

ASSERTIVENESS

Never be afraid to speak your mind. Speaking your mind is now so widely accepted that you can pay to learn how to do it. This makes me laugh. People say to me, 'Why are you so aggressive?' I say to them, 'Why are you so short?' There is apparently a fine line between aggression and assertiveness but I would be more wary of the line between being assertive and sounding like a spoilt brat. It's a tiny one, especially in restaurants.

KNOWING AND GETTING WHAT YOU WANT OTHER THAN A JOB

Pretty well all the above applies. Use your common sense.

Rule: *Always speak distinctly. Then when you tell people what you want they won't say, 'Sorry, I missed all that. You'll have to start again.'*

GETTING TO THE TOP

What is the top? That's the question. And how do you know when you're there? People who strive are never satisfied, even when they are straddling Everest, industry or the local branch of Boots. They might know they can go no higher on this particular mountain range but all that means is they must find something else to conquer. I like that about striving. I strongly advise you to strive. But find a top you can call your own.

Career structures are all very well for the that-way-inclined but have you seen them? They are made of straw in this day of the short-term contract and you can topple off over and over again through no fault of your own. You might get shoved, a rung might collapse beneath you, or you might just get fed up using a whole lot of energy on stuff that has nothing to do with the job you like. Structures don't recognise true worth either. I have always avoided them.

COMPETITION

This could be because I am overcompetitive or undercompetitive. Maybe it's fearfulness of competition, fearfulness of what I become when competing or fear of failure. Who cares? The point is knowing where you work best. For me, that's at home with one eye over my shoulder for younger, cleverer people I will never have to meet.

You, on the other hand, may flourish in the face of immediate competition and relish the neck and neckness of it all. Just watch out for people who play dirty. They will subvert your best efforts, refuse to involve you and try to make you look incompetent, like the cows at school. Deal with them however you see fit though not by punching or you will end up in court.

Competition is currently back in fashion because it's said to bring out the best in people. It is currently not the thing to ackowledge it also brings out the worst. Speaking for myself, I'd rather lift my game on my own account than for the sake of thrashing someone else into the ground and I would suggest you do the same. This isn't to say you can't delight in someone else's lacklustre performance. Of course you can. I do all the time.

LIMITATIONS AND THE FOLLY
OF RECOGNISING THEM

Someone once said to me, 'What I like about you is you know you'll never be another Ralph Nader.' Even then I had to laugh. 'Ralph who?' you will be saying. Precisely. Ralph Nader was a consumer campaigner who peaked in the seventies.

Why would I ever have aspired to be a Ralph Nader?

It's a terrible mistake to define your aspirations in terms of anyone else, alive or dead, let alone accept you'll never reach anyone else's dizzying heights in the field of customers' rights. Not only would I never admit Ralph Nader into my focus, I wouldn't even include William Thackeray or Elaine May, and I admire them hugely.

You want to be whoever you are going to become and you should do your darnedest to be whoever that person is. Give it your all but make it *your* all, not blinking Ralph's.

Rule: There is no top. Just a succession of peaks which come with troughs. Never be beaten by a trough. The very next peak could be the big one.

WHERE GENDER
GETS YOU

WHAT IT MEANS
TO BE A WOMAN

Two things about being a woman cast everything else into the outer suburbs of who cares city. They are wanting to have sex with men and having a body which, after having sex with men, can produce babies. You might also enjoy belonging to a sisterhood whose inherited memory may or may not include spells and potions though you must please yourself on that one.

If I hadn't wanted to have sex with men and had periods, a bosom and babies, I might just as well have been your father though smaller and a little bit less tidy. There remain many people who don't believe this. You will meet them from time to time and they will get right up your nose. Should anyone say, 'You do it. You're a woman,' and they're not talking about having a baby, the correct response is, 'Drop dead, sponge bag.'

IDIOTS

We know people like this. They think I am a bossy, domineering, controlling cow and your father is a saint and they have deduced this on the scant evidence of their own eyes. They will die unhappy, trapped in the putrid dungeon of their neurotically rigid thinking. You know very well that your father and I nearly always like and want the same things. I just happen to like and want them first.

These ridiculous people think I get my own way by shouting. If your father liked and wanted things first, if it looked as if his will was being imposed upon the family, they would be happy because they think this is the natural order. Let me tell you, if we'd had to hang about waiting for their natural order to triumph, you wouldn't be here. You'd be in Palmers Green N13 where your father and I began married life and I threw up from too many houses looking the same. Your father would argue we would also not be in debt but I would rather be in debt than in Palmers Green, and in his heart he agrees with me.

A BARMY TEST

When you were small and I was researching my rape book, we found a test designed to show how masculine or feminine we were. Femininity was emotional, vulnerable and caring etc. Masculinity was logical, single-minded and aggressive etc. I came out highly masculine and your father came out averagely feminine.

Your father is a large man who has in his time been a rugby forward, a boxer, a mountain climber and a motorbike racer. He has had to punch strangers in the street in road rage incidents. I have never been or done any of those things yet they are all kind of butch. So what are they saying? This is a fact: gender has nothing to do with personality. It is simply a question of build and hormones.

HORMONES

Until I was about thirteen, I wanted to be a boy. I wasn't the only one. You were mad if you didn't. Boys ran everything, like street games, Monopoly and most conversations. They also kept the horde of cigarettes we nicked from our parents which were Ardaths and Craven A cork tipped. They swaggered about the place looking rough, tough, in charge and superior. Girly behaviour was so uneventful that some girls who didn't want to be boys pretended to be horses but I could never get into that.

Having periods changed everything. Hormones surged around my body, skinny and odd-looking though it was, and I never wanted to be a boy again, only to have as many as possible drooling over me with lust and adoration, which was a forlorn hope.

You have never shown any signs of wanting to be boys, except for one of you wanting to be called Big Jim when you were two but that was about truck driving. This could be because you are gorgeous but it's more likely that being a boy isn't so wonderful any more. Everyone is suffering from a failure of gender expectations owing to where we are in history.

GENDER EXPECTATIONS

Since the sixties when girls got to keep their own Ardaths, the state of play between women and men has been a quagmire of unanswerable questions. If men aren't heads of the household, should they still be knights in shining armour? If women earn as much as men and work out three times a week, what's the point in mascara? That kind of thing.

I will try to guide you through this mess. The solution is to forget gender; think about sex.

SEX

Getting men to want to have sex with you is the best fun you will ever have. It's why we practise from birth – displaying everywhere like Andrew the peacock in next door's garden in Sydney – and what we end up with is femininity. Femininity is designed to attract men.

All three of you have been famously flirtatious, even in your Big Jim days. It will be instinct, I suppose. The important thing for you to remember, however, is that it's a game and not to be confused with the rest of your life.

THE TUNDRA

We know this because the mating rituals are different in different parts of the world and change according to cultural need. They won't be the same in the tundra. I don't know what they get up to in the tundra. In our part of the world, they are to do with the men being protectors and providers and women being home-makers even though men are no longer expected to protect and provide or women to home-make. It's tradition based on old fashioned economics.

You don't have to be tiny, or even soft and curvy to be feminine, though this is a popular look. You simply have to suggest vulnerability now and again. Only suggest, mind you. It's silly to carry it too far. Who really wants to have their food ordered for them all their lives? And be bossed about by someone who turns out to know a whole lot less and be a whole lot less competent?

Here are some suggestions for looking vulnerable on a casual basis: 1) ask advice as if you mean it; 2) fall over now and again; 3) squint. That's enough.

LESBIANS

There are women who only want to have sex with other women and they are no less women. Well, maybe a little bit less, I don't know. You may be one of them. I know you keep saying you're not but I just want to assure you one more time that I have positively no problem if you are. Nor has your father. He is, after all, the man who stood outside the bathroom door with a Lillets diagram in his hand when one of you had an unfortunate incident with a tampon. All I'm saying is, if you're gay, you're gay.

I have only liked sex with men and everything about you suggests you are the same. I don't really know what lesbians get up to in bed but someone who does says it's exactly like straight sex only the plumbing's different.

CELIBACY

You might also be a woman who isn't much interested in sex. That's OK. Our drives are all different. Or you might be extra interested but unable to pursue it because you are phobic. That's also OK. Get help (see earlier). But just to make myself clear, if you are a) not at all interested, as a woman you will not behave in the same way as you would if you were b) phobic.

Being a woman, as opposed to being a regular person who goes about her day to day business in a regular fashion, is only really significant when it comes to courting rituals. If you're not interested in the courting rituals, being a woman will be neither here nor there though you may still be reminded of it on a monthly basis.

PERIODS

Periods are a complete pain in the butt, though more so for some than for others. When I first had mine, Mrs Thompson from along the road warned me they would last a very long time and I would never get to like them; this was her line on the whole of human life. She was right about periods though. In those days sanitary towels were like plaster casts that you wore between your legs and they ripped all your flesh off as well as leaked.

Things have improved out of sight with tampons but you must be vigilant in this respect. Some women forget what's up there, keep reloading and end up with toxic shock or in hospital consulting a doctor who needs to go in there with a torch.

Be careful, also, about chronic irregularity which is

in the family. It can affect fertility but it doesn't always. Fertility and infertility are notoriously difficult to pick and we have a very lovely granddaughter to prove it.

PUBLIC DISPLAYS OF PERIOD PAIN

Some men love the idea of women getting the vapours when they have a period. Then sneer about women's failure to cope at certain times of the month as if they would whistle with searing pains in the stomach, back and legs and chronic blood loss every four weeks. It's my view they sneer because they imagine periods give us magic powers. In dealing with such pig-like men, I advise you to do that curse about the coffee grains and make their hair fall out.

PMT

Your grandmother says PMT doesn't exist. We were certainly never allowed to have it and I don't. But there's no doubt lots of women do and sometimes one or other of you says you do. This is jolly bad luck. I wouldn't dwell on it. There are things you can take to even out your hormones. I don't know what they are. See a doctor.

CHILDBIRTH

There is much argument as to how much carrying and bearing children separates women from men. Does it render women more able to tolerate pain, give them a greater sense of destiny, make them more immediately and inextricably bonded to their children? Maybe. We are in a cultural flux. With fathers being that much more involved in the process, time could possibly tell.

I do know that your father assumed I knew more about babies than he did simply because you had been inside me, and although I yelled at him for being such a prat, I also encouraged it. I like to have that privileged position in your lives, even if it is fraudulent.

Once I had babies, what it meant to be a woman changed gear for me completely. Wanting to attract men I could sleep with became that much less urgent. More than anything else it meant being a mother and being a mother meant being completely enslaved to the needs and happiness of my children. I'm not saying I didn't have a life. I did in a funny sort of way. But you were, and remain, paramount in it. The same went for your father but it was different and I think it was different because he was a man.

Rule: Your father says if you are ever called upon to punch, keep your thumb outside your fist and your centre knuckle sticking out. His friend Bubbles says only girls punch with their thumbs inside the fist and so their thumbs break. Only punch if you can get away with it.

WHAT YOU NEED
TO KNOW ABOUT MEN

Men make excellent partners for life. They aren't always handy with a Black and Decker but that's the way of it these days. They can be loving, considerate, helpful and on your side which is enough long-term. There are certain things you need to know about them, however, before you commit yourself to one for any length of time.

As a result of being in charge of everything for so long, some men behave like lunatics. This behaviour, in a partner for life, is so grim you have to lash out and if that doesn't work, you must pretend they are dead.

A ROUGH GUIDE TO CURIOUS
MALE BEHAVIOUR

For a start, there's this ridiculous need to be handled with kid gloves. You will hear women say things like, 'Don't speak to your father until he's eaten.' Or, 'Ask him when he's wearing his yellow trousers.' I have never done it and I believe fewer and fewer women are doing it because it's so demeaning all round. But some men have been raised to it. They will be reluctant to abandon their position of privilege so they will flinch, look amazed and ask to be left alone in times of stress, noise or unexpected visitors.

There is also male-pattern deafness which is men only hearing what they want to hear. You will recognise it by the silly facial expression which says, 'I am not hearing you.' It will occur in times of emergency as in, 'Could you please answer the phone', and everyday living, 'Has anyone seen the salt?' It also occurs when they are at the foot of the stairs and you are halfway up with a piano on your back, the reason being you should not expect them to come to you.

As well, you will come across unfamiliarity with other people's possessions. Few men ever know where anything is if they don't own it. This is why they can never put away the washing in a house with more than two people in it or find anything in the kitchen.

Most astonishing of all, however, is their ability to think only one thought after the other. This is called linear thinking. The great philosophers may be different but I've never met any. Rarely do you spot a man doing more than one thing at a time. When you ask him to spare you a minute he'll say, 'Hang on, I'm doing something,' as if what he's doing will shift the globe on its axis. He'll go, 'I'm watching television' or 'I'm just drinking my tea.'

Linear thinking would seem to suggest a paltry intellectual capacity, but there is nothing wrong with the average male capacity for thought, just in his capacity for putting himself out. Most women do it instinctively but it's probably time they stopped, unless they are thinking of the common good.

MARKED IMPROVEMENT

Men are changing and women are changing because life is changing. I don't suppose we will ever take on the mores of the tundra, but we will take on the mores of a two-income family in which the partners are equally well-educated and free to make the same choices about commitment. This will eventually have a large impact on learnt behaviour.

Your father, despite his selective hearing, is ahead of the pack. The reason is simple. He is a man who likes women. He enjoys the company of women. He is full of admiration for women and he listens with interest to what they have to say, unlike the manifold jerks who imagine a woman's greatest pleasure is listening to them. He isn't full of macho bull dust. How lucky that at seventeen I saw that. Even he, however, has had his erratic moments, especially when I was seventeen.

AN INCIDENT FROM MY LIFE WHICH SHOWS YOUR FATHER IN AN ODD LIGHT

When I was about seventeen, your father and I were driving down the main street of a suburban shopping centre and he enquired after my make-up which was the usual – much eye, little lip and something for the bones. He wanted to know why I was wearing any. I said because I liked to, which couldn't have been simpler. He said why did I like to. I said because it made me feel more attractive. He said why did I want to look attractive. I said because everyone did. He said it could only be for other men, since he was already attracted to me, and what was I doing trying to attract other men when he had already proposed to me.

The conversation grew very heated, centring on the rights of the individual. One thing led to another and I believe I slapped him outside the greengrocer's. We aren't talking protector/provider here. This was proprietor. Utter madness. Your father was always a man of passion but you have to watch out for that ownership thing. Yuk!

Today's young man understands that but he tends to be covered in confusion, owing to balls being in the air, so to speak.

But not fast enough

The main source of confusion is where he stands. If he is no longer required to protect and provide, what is he expected to do? Talk about slow! Why can't he get to grips with the idea that romance isn't real life but needs to be accommodated just the same?

It's all very well to accept women on equal terms and to treat them with the same respect they treat a mate, but women require something beyond mateship. They want a little role-playing, a little gender differentiation. They want romance. They want to be seduced even if they do control mighty empires. It's called a double standard. Not too complicated I think. Life is riddled with them.

My advice to you is to look for a man with a little chivalry up his sleeve. This is a man who will understand and respect your brain, your right to choice and your independence, but will also understand that there is nothing more glorious for a woman than a man's well-muscled arm round her waist, implying strength, lust and pleasure in her and her alone.

The general problem seems to be confusion of signals. And how easily they are confused.

AN EXAMPLE FROM THE ANIMAL KINGDOM

There was poor old Andrew the peacock, desperate for a hen, quite attractive in a birdy kind of way, displaying everywhere and someone poisoned him. One person's signal is another person's terrible shouting. Practise your expressions. Try to make them as unambiguous as possible.

EVEN WORSE

The hesitant man, however, is a whole pile better than the man who imagines his gender has bestowed upon him overwhelming sexual urges which women are just longing, and must expect, to have directed at them. This is the man who thinks with his penis. The technical name for him is dickhead.

PENISES AND HOW THEY AFFECT WHAT YOU WEAR

There are many dickheads about and they are the reason I bolt the door when I see you leaving the house wrapped in a handkerchief. I respect your right to leave the house in a handkerchief. Not so long ago, I was a devotee of the handkerchief as a skirt myself. I respect your right to look like a sex goddess but I respect even more your safety.

Out there are men who truly think that because

you are wearing a handkerchief you are inviting them specifically to have intercourse with you. They know they are lying to themselves but their penises persuade them.

You know and I know that, though your intention is to look attractive and possibly like a sex goddess, this is not an invitation to sick remarks and groping. They, however, tell themselves that sex goddesses expect to be the object of sick remarks and groping, especially as performed by them, because women in handkerchiefs are begging for it. These are immature, gormless creatures and they are why you must never leave the house looking like anyone who can be confused with a tart.

Save the hanky for places of safety but keep in mind that, even then, there are men with penises for brains who don't understand that how you look is an invitation to nothing except admiration which is best left unsaid if it can't be said nicely. Bear in mind that anything can be provocative to the man who delights in his overpowering sexual urges. Even a white shirt buttoned to the collar, so for him, hanky most definitely equals panky.

A sense of proportion here: only the very odd lech is dangerous but he is the one a mother fears. The rule under all circumstances, whether the lech looks harmless or not, is to allow nothing in your manner to suggest he is on to a good thing. Put him straight as soon and as definitely as you can and remove yourself from his presence. If you must wear a handkerchief on the Tube, wear it under a raincoat.

THE HARMLESS LECH

It is ridiculous to sue him for sexual harassment. He can be seen off very simply and should be.

THE TROUBLESOME LECH

Should a man use his position of authority to foist unwelcome sexual attention upon you, you must take evasive action. Never allow yourself to be alone with him. When there are witnesses, you must complain very loudly and very publicly. Where there are no witnesses, knee him and run. (See rule on punching earlier.)

KNOWING WHAT'S WHAT

The truth is that you have to take responsibility for your own safety and comfort. However much you believe you are entitled to walk down the road by yourself at night and wear dresses cut entirely for suggestion, only a complete idiot of a daughter would. Only an idiot would jump into a cage of hungry lions smothered in Whiskas. Listen to what I'm saying. It's important.

Dickheads are not a reason, however, for thinking you should play down your beauty. You are entitled to make the most of yourself. I would even go so far as to say obliged. Who wants to die unnoticed?

Rule: *Do not commit yourself to a partner for life who has low blood sugar rendering him incapable of any kind of thinking before food.*

MEN AS FRIENDS

I love my men friends. Never are they as much fun as they are at your age. Any minute now, most of them will become self-important, married and dull but single men friends are fun and easy, as well as more reliable than girlfriends once you've sorted out the sexual tension.

There will always be some sort of sexual tension between you and men, not only because you are vibrantly attractive and flirtatious by nature, but because there always is between men and women. Or have I been kidding myself all this time?

FANCYING

I'm not talking about attraction, just the awareness that attraction could exist on account of you being of the opposite sex; one of you or both of you might be having lascivious thoughts. You have to deal with this.

Sometimes this awareness is very slight, as in 'Is he standing close or am I getting fat?' or only on your side, as in 'Cor!' Sometimes one or other of you neglects to

acknowledge it and it crops up when least expected.
You have to deal with it before a friendship can
settle down.

DEALING WITH SEXUAL TENSION –
SOME EXAMPLES

You don't have to agonise over it. You don't even need
to mention it outright. You just have to indicate with a
line, an anecdote or gesture where you stand for the
time being. *A discouraging line:* my boyfriend comes
out of jail tomorrow; I go everywhere with my mother.
A distancing anecdote: my teeth are so rotten that the
dentist has to use a room freshener when I leave. *Some
non-sexual gestures:* throwing up; coughing without
covering your mouth; hard back-slapping.

HOW TO PROCEED

It doesn't mean you can't flirt. It just means you both
know the flirting is pretend. If that doesn't suit both
of you then there won't be a friendship. It'll just be a
romance that didn't happen.

Everything can change, of course. There's a song
about making lovers of friends. But what you need to
establish is what's what for the time being.

BUT HOW GOOD ARE THEY?

In childhood, boys make much better friends for
girls than other girls. They are less complicated, less
competitive and far more accepting of what's said and

done at face value. There's none of this scheming that girls get up to while they are working out their pecking order. All this changes at around twelve or thirteen when thoughts of a sexual nature barge into everything completely uninvited. Then it's almost impossible to have friendships with boys which have no sexual component of any sort.

Even if you think the fellow is just a good mate and tell everyone he's just a good mate and he agrees he's just a good mate, he could be biding his time. Or you could just be biding yours. Biding doesn't matter all that much, unless it becomes too obvious and irritating. He can still be a great friend, listening to your woes, offering to defend you to the death and having a great laugh but he might suddenly take it upon himself to feel spurned and withdraw the friendship. Testosterone can do that.

Girlfriends are at their least reliable at this time so any kind of loyalty and affection should be respected and appreciated.

At this age, it's also very hard for ex-boyfriends to remain friends even though girls always say that is what they would like. Someone's ego has usually been too badly bashed about for early recovery. Later, after university say, it's a little better. But even quite grown-up exes can drive you mad by being smug and know-all when things go wrong for you.

SOMETHING FUNNY

It's spookily popular right now for boys and girls to sleep together without having sex just for comfort, warmth and convenience. One or other might say, 'You can sleep with me, if you like.' And the impression they like to give is that sex is out of the question but excuse me? Of course sex is the question. What's going on here is a testing of the water to see if natural impulses transcend fear of rejection. Never go to bed with a boy unless you have a condom handy. Natural impulses can't be relied upon to remain dormant, no matter how matey or frightened of rejection either or both of you are.

That said, there's no denying this generation of boys is quite good at friendship. They've been brought up not to treat all women as sex objects and to feel comfortable with displays of affection which are mostly devoid of lust.

It has created a tricky kind of no man's land, however, between friendship and romance, which can be very difficult to negotiate for both sexes. There might be mutual fancying but no one wants to move on anyone in case all that's on offer is friendship and there's a ghastly moment of reckoning when the person moved on moves away in embarrassment. Look at the dramas we've had in this house.

PRIDE

Boys who act like friends then move on you might be after a romance. But more likely they are after sex and think it is fine to have sex with girls who are friends without commitment. This may be fine by you, but almost certainly not.

If it's romance you are after and not uncommitted sex with friendship, I don't think a serious declaration of intent can go astray, even if it does mean laying your pride on the line. Someone has to do it sooner or later. Make your pride a flexible thing.

OTHER MEN

Once you are in a relationship, your partner will be suspicious of all men friends who aren't his as well. And even then, he will be suspicious of any suggestion that the friendship with his friends is growing independently of him. This is unfair and irritating and you can fight the battle if you want to but be prepared for men friends to say you're no fun any more or for your partner to call you unfaithful.

Now is the time to cultivate your women friends. They will be in the same boat and this is a bonding thing.

Rule: *Boys who pretend to be friends but try to stick their hands down your trousers aren't friends.*

WOMEN AS FRIENDS

Until the last ten years or so, I used to think I was a man's woman. Kind of Lauren Bacallish. I despised girly talk even if there was a lot of dungaree involved. I thought women's rights were so obvious that to have to argue the justice of them was demeaning.

I loved the fact that men were happy to debate serious issues with me; that we read the same bits of newspapers and liked the same books. I don't know what all that was about now. Sex? I suppose it was sex. One way or another. Most things seem to be.

For years, the only women I comfortably discussed issues with were my sisters. I can't believe that all the women I like now weren't up for the same conversations. Maybe they were busy having them with men as well and it was a kind of intellectual flirtation that made everyone feel clever and important. Maybe it took me longer than usual to recover from the horror of girls at school.

SCHOOLFRIENDS – MINE

Here is a memory from school: I am on the train with three or four girls in my class and they are laughing and chatting with boys from a nearby school, several of whom they have kissed. I have kissed nobody so I just stand next to them, looking involved yet geeky. When we get off the train, one of the girls who is known throughout several schools for her sex appeal says to me, 'When we're with boys why do you just stand there grinning and looking stupid?'

About eight years later, this girl arrives in London where I am living. She has a husband who is a solicitor and nice enough but a bit dull. I have been married for ages and no longer care less about grinning in the company of the opposite sex. I engage her husband in some sort of lively debate because that was what I did in those days for a good time and she says in astonishment, 'Barbara, you don't think you're Pete's equal, do you?' I laughed and laughed.

How weird she had never noticed my intellectual pretensions. I came from a family who had no television except in the holidays, wasn't allowed to listen to commercial radio, and followed the cricket. Maybe she was fooled by my inadequate progress at school or maybe she thought I was like everyone else who wanted to be sexy and had cultivated an intellect the size of a pea. I kept no friends from school.

I'm telling you this so you can see how things change. I now have many excellent and valued women friends. Some I have kept for thirty years. There is no disputing that women as friends improve with age.

You

You have formed better friendships at school and the two of you who have left have kept a handful which is astonishing to me but apparently normal. I would still be failing you if I didn't pinpoint a few types of whom you should be wary.

Types of friends

The girl who wants to be like you; the girl who thinks you want to be like her; the girl who can only feel good about herself by making you feel terrible; the girl who thinks she's doing you a favour by pulling you down a peg or two; the girl who can't get by without you except when she has someone better to get by with; the girl who would put herself out for you only she really has other things she has to see to first like her clothes; and the girl who likes you but . . .

They can all make perfectly reasonable friends. They can be kind, sensitive, loyal and fun but not all the time. You just need to understand the limits of their friendship. All but a very few are limited; it doesn't make them not worth having. The older you get the less you care about the limits. You have different friends for different reasons and it is perfectly sensible to replace those who drop by the wayside.

Making friends

This becomes much easier once you have children. Many of our friends are the parents of children you went to school with. Parenthood is a bonding thing in itself but so is school. Isn't that mad when school has, in another life, been so friend-free? Once you are a parent, you only have to stand in a queue of other parents and yawn to strike up a new friendship.

Once, when I felt I could do with another cool, well-dressed woman friend with a lively expression and endearing laugh, I decided to move in on this mother of two pretty daughters. I sidled up to her one afternoon, caught her eye and said, 'Been for a swim?' She looked puzzled. 'No, dirty hair,' she said. A little while later, completely confident that we now had a rich seam of shared waiting to explore I said, 'Oh, you're pregnant.' She examined me with interest. 'No,' she said. 'I'm just fat.' She became my friend anyway but I think I always liked her more than she liked me and after a while she drifted away.

Friends of both sexes do that but women, I find, are very good at keeping up. You must be as well. Many of the competitive prickles in female friendships fall off as their bloom fades. Then we cleave to each other to laugh about fading sex appeal and to find our amusement elsewhere. By the time you get to my age, you will have endless happy hours in their company, cackling like crones, discussing issues and wondering why our husbands don't have friends like we do.

Rule: *The reason husbands don't have friends like women do is because men like to talk about themselves and women like to talk about everybody else.*

LOVE, SEX AND MARRIAGE

LOVE

M ost of what you know about love you will have
learnt from songs and just about now you will be
discovering what a swizz that is. The failure of reality
to match the lyrics is sometimes very disheartening.
You can, if you so choose, reinvent the disappointing
object of your heart's desire.

In your fantasy life you could, for example, turn
him into the boy I first introduced you to via song and
gesture when you were tiny; the one up in the balcony.
'There he is awaving of his han'kerchee, as carefree
as a robin, that sits upon a tree.' What a lad. No one
could blame you. And it's easily done. You just have
to wander around saying, 'Isn't he just like the boy up
in the balcony? Have you seen the way he looks down
at me?'

But I would advise against it. Sooner or later,
reality will rear its ugly head grimly and you will
be forced to acknowledge that the man whose
attention you have been pining for isn't actually
looking down at you at all but at the ice-cream tray
and he is salivating. Better this happens sooner,
so you can appreciate that what you have had here

is a brief romance only and nothing to break your heart over.

I don't know why popular culture nurtures such false expectations. Where is the song that says, 'I only love you 'cos you love me' when this is plainly the truth of it? Love, in the first instance, is an overwhelming sense of relief and joy that someone not too revolting has fallen for you.

Lust

This is what confuses the issue. How easy is it to drool over someone who never gives you a second glance? It's just as easy to catch someone's eye across an embarrassingly poor turn-out and know at once with a dreadful lurch of your stomach and curl of your lip that you fancy the pants off each other. Boredom is a great whetter of that kind of appetite. Being unable to keep your hands off someone has positively nothing to do with loving them, however.

Loving is the emotion that will sustain you through fifty years of living under the one roof, watching each other breathe and listening to each other eat. It can be but isn't necessarily part of the chain that leads to the golden wedding party where two other young people will catch each other's eyes and smirk in mutual recognition. Here, for your edification, is how the chain works.

LUST BUT DIFFERENT

You meet someone and fancy him. This can be mutual or it might be one-sided. He might fancy you and you might think 'what a nice guy' of him. Either way, one of you has a strong physical interest in the other and the other isn't completely indifferent. The one with the interest pursues it with the necessary amount of vigour, rousing the interest of the not entirely uninterested party and quite soon, in the popular vernacular, you get it on. This will involve passionate kissing at the very least and, depending on how everything else is going, could move on to very much more.

ROMANCE

It is perfectly possible to enjoy a really good snog with someone you don't much like, but only once or twice. With luck, in between the snogging, you will be speaking to each other and establishing some kind of mental connection which will involve recognition of mutual interests, hopes, expectations and things you find funny.

This will give a whole new dimension to the relationship and hope for the future, be it ever so short. During this period you will enjoy each other's company and in between the snogging etc. try to spend as much time in it as possible. When you are not together you might feel sick with longing. This is a good sign but doesn't necessarily mean anything significant long-term is happening. Lust and delight in the romance can play funny tricks on judgement.

EMBELLISHING

If you find to your dismay you don't have all that much
in common, you will inevitably invest this excellent
snogger and very desirable body with a personality
he doesn't have but which justifies his presence in
your life. Your friends and family will go along with it
because they will be happy you have found someone
to snog after such a long drought but they will always
have a flat expression in their voice and eyes so that
you will repeatedly hear yourself saying: 'He's nice,
isn't he?' and 'You don't really like him, do you? It's
only because you don't know him.'

SO?

This is OK short-term. It's even brilliant, short-term. It's
the nature of most romances. But when it goes on for
many months it becomes terrible to watch. You become
an object of pity and ridicule. Should this occur in any
of your cases, I will employ a cult-buster to kidnap you
and have you de-programmed.

There is no greater folly than to succumb to a
physical addiction for a man whose temperament will
one way or another do you in long-term. This addiction
is called 'unhealthy fixation' and many women are
prone to it for reasons I have never attempted to
fathom. They must be victims. I have no patience with
the victim mentality. They tell themselves they can't
help it. They are in love. But they aren't in love. They
are dependent. They should embark on a twelve-step
plan to break the dependency.

FALLING IN LOVE

This is best achieved when there is enormous affection on both sides and a strong mental connection. The lust quotient doesn't have to be equal – it will vary anyway, depending on spots, hormones and feelings of panic. One partner might be full of lust and the other only half full but this is enough. Both the lust and liking grow immeasurably when it is recognised to be mutual. There is nothing quite so adorable in a man you like and fancy as him loving you to death. To be loved is the most endearing thing on earth, provided it's not by a creep or a stalker.

WARTS

After a while, no matter how much fancying, liking and loving is going on, tiny shafts of light will fall on certain aspects of a man's personality which will give you cause for thought. He might, for instance, have a shoe fetish. I don't mean a sexual one. I mean a shopping one. Perhaps he must constantly buy shoes because he is vain about his feet. This is all very well in a romance but what does it say long-term? What are the implications of a shoe fetish in a partner for life? You have to ask yourself these questions. Does it mean he's a bore? A maniac? A spendthrift? A little bit stupid? And if it means any of the above, can this be tolerated? I cannot stress too much the importance of appreciating your tolerance threshold in any relationship.

LOVE

Enduring love, as distinct from the thing you fall into, is based on mutual respect as well as all the stuff I said before. And you need it. Boy, do you need it. Even when you truly love someone and say to yourself you love them warts and all, there will be trouble. That is when mutual respect is all that can save you.

In every relationship there are bones of contention on which one or other of you, if not both, will gag at regular intervals. They are there because you have different mothers and fathers and different egos. You must decide whether or not you can gag, recover and move on. Acceptance is everything in love long term and will be the governing factor long after desire has subsided and liking is no longer an issue. Acceptance and mutual respect. This is what you will be looking for long term.

LOSERS

Apart from investing your time and affection in an unsuitable love object, you may be tempted to invest them in someone who has positively no interest in you and may not even know you live. This is called unrequited love and it is as helpful in your life as black death. To pine after someone who doesn't appreciate your pining is nuts. Some people, of course, hang in there for many years and eventually their love object hits his head in a kitchen fall and wakes up crying, 'I've been a mad fool. Marry me.' Don't hold your breath. Get cognitive therapy.

SHOULD YOU GET DUMPED

A boy who dumps you isn't worth knowing. He
will be either blind or ignorant or both, threatened
by your great beauty or mammoth intelligence and
uncomfortable with a family as close as we are. What a
sap. Forget him. You'll say it's not as easy as that and
he has redeeming features or he wouldn't have been
your boyfriend in the first place. But I'm telling you.
I don't want to hear about his great shoulders or his
sultry eyes. They are as nothing. He is gone.

Don't mope. Don't pine. Losers mope and pine.
Be very sad for a day or two, write a couple of sad
poems, feel outraged and move on. Tell everyone you
were dumped because that's better than having them
whisper it behind your back and if you see him again,
be gracious but don't be fooled. If it didn't work once, I
can't think of a reason it might work another time.

MY LOVE LIFE

I have had one love interest in my life and he is your
father. You have seen how we carry on. That's about
the sum of it.

*Rule: If you get to be forty-one and you are still pining for a
mysterious dark-haired man, people will think you're crazy
and rightly call you Delta Dawn.*

SEX

You know how to have sex. A man puts his penis into the woman's vagina and after a while he ejaculates into a condom. I don't want to hear about sex without a condom. Well, I do, but only so I can get you counselling.

There will come a time, of course, when you will know the man well enough to get by without a condom. By then you may be thinking about having his baby because you will be in a rock-solid relationship and you'll be one hundred per cent sure that he doesn't have Aids or any other sexually transmittable disease. But until then, the main thing you need to know about sex is how to have it safely so you can rest easy every month.

You think this isn't very romantic? Why would I be romantic about something like this? I'm your mother. The position of the mother regarding sex is entirely missionary. You don't want sex to make you ill and you don't want sex to make you pregnant unless you're ready for a baby and all that that entails.

WHEN TO HAVE IT

This will be a personal matter. I have already told you having it too young, or too often too young, will hurt and give you cancer as well as great heartache. This is a personal view and you can put it out of your mind once you've left school when it will cease to apply.

The fashion is no longer to have it as often as possible with as many different people as possible though you do still meet the occasional unhappy person who can't help themselves. They're sad in my experience but this could be because having endless sexual partners has never been my experience which is unusually limited for a woman of my age and inclinations.

I don't see anything wrong with the principle of recreational sex, by which I mean one-night stands with men you hardly know, I just don't know how brilliant it is afterwards. That's the thing about sex. There's the before sex, the doing it and the after sex and each element is as important as the other.

As far as I can tell, most women think the after bit is as important as the it bit, so my advice would be to think ahead a tiny amount before you leap into bed with someone. How slight the relationship can be for comfort will be your judgement but you should take self-preservation into account in the broadest sense of the term.

For a decent afterglow, trust is much, much more important than lust. You want someone who will have consideration for your finer feelings, physical and emotional, and your good name. I know reputations for promiscuity aren't supposed to count any more but it seems to me you won't feel too bright about yourself if everyone thinks you're a slapper.

You want affection and warmth as well as great sex

and I'm not sure you're going to get that with someone you've only known for a minute and whose interest in you is entirely physical. A man whose interest in you is entirely physical will be entirely interested in himself. Forget him. You may definitely call me old-fashioned on this one.

What you don't need to become is one of those people who must have sex with lots of partners just to feel good about herself because love and affection is lacking in your life and you feel ugly. Should you ever meet such a crisis, I would expect you to come to me, your father or one of your sisters and we will be able to remind you how loved you are and perhaps get you some bromide.

HOW TO SEDUCE

Opportunities for this will rarely crop up since most men you fancy will fancy you and Bob will be your uncle. Occasionally, however, you will fix your attention on a man who seems oblivious of your charms and you will want to test the depth of this oblivion. Hanging around blushing, shaking and perspiring is one way of going about it but I've never seen it work. I don't believe anything does as well as brazen. This begins with prolonged eye contact and incidental brushing against. Then you go right up to the jerk who's pretending you are a door and you say, 'How about it then?' I have explained this to you on many occasions and you have all fled from the room screaming and claiming I am not your mother. But try it. Truly.

BEING GOOD AT IT

With luck, you will all have sex for the first time with boys who love you and this will set you up for life. But if you don't, it's not a catastrophe, just an unfortunate episode and life is full of them. You move on. Don't allow the memory to affect your sex life for ever because sex is one of the great wonders of human experience and the last thing you need is to have emotional scars ruin it for you. Also, ignore lovers who make you feel inadequate. Everyone's great at sex with the right person. And just because he likes it swinging from a rafter doesn't mean anyone else does.

Athleticism and inventiveness are all very well if you're being paid but if you're being paid, something has to compensate for lust, warmth and affection. You're as good at it as the moment allows and some moments there will be no one better on earth. Moving, of course, helps. The woman lying perfectly still works only for some men.

Don't ever have sex for money; don't ever do stuff that repels you; if you don't want to have sex, say you don't, even when you are married.

THE NATIONAL AVERAGE

Once you are married, you might feel pressured to have sex in keeping with the national average which I believe is twice a week. Twice a week can be twice a week too many for some couples and twice a week too few for others. Unless you have an unnatural sexual appetite yourself, avoid marrying a man who does.

CONTRACEPTION

Take responsibility for this yourself because you are
the one who will become pregnant if you don't. Always
use a condom in the early days of a relationship. And
go on the pill. I say that only because it is simple.
The pill doesn't agree with everyone and you will
probably spend a great deal of time thinking you have
thrombosis. Even so, I preferred it to the diaphragm.
I could never get on with the diaphragm. There was
something about the tension and insertion. I would
lose my grip and it would go pinging around the
bedroom which was only so-so for passion. Get expert
contraceptive advice and stick with it. If you become
pregnant, tell me.

HOW I BECAME A GRANDMOTHER

No one has a second's regret about it now but at the
time it wasn't easy. There was your sister, newly in
love, newly moved in with her boyfriend and about to
start her BSc when suddenly she was struck down by
terrible stomach cramps and a high fever. She came
home and we summoned doctors from everywhere
who advised a scan. The GP said it showed she had an
ovarian condition which meant she was infertile but she
would do some hormone tests which would with luck
show it could be treated.

Your sister was distraught. To cheer her up I said to
look on the bright side (see The Right Attitude earlier).
She could sling out all her troublesome contraception.
She was pregnant within the week. Your auntie says
it had nothing to do with the GP or the scan. Someone
was bound to get pregnant because I had planted

parsley. There is no moral to this story. The baby has been the greatest argument against contraception ever. Even so, other bundles of joy could be ruder shocks.

Guilt

I know I have put the case firmly against having sex too early. This was only out of concern for your emotional and physical welfare which is always paramount in my mind and sex is one of the rare areas in your life when I can't actually be there for you. The important thing is that you should enjoy it. There are books available if you don't.

Rule: If you have trouble saying 'I love you', use a foreign accent. It worked for your father.

THE PERFECT PARTNER

Y ou will only know if you have found the perfect
partner if he survives the test of time. And time
begins its test the minute you meet. You might meet,
you might part, you might not see each other for years,
then you might collide in Tesco's and eventually marry
when you'd have sworn that a man who bought only
own-brand products was the last person you'd end
up with.

The perfect partnership is no more than a
comfortable arrangement as I have told you over and
over again. Ridiculous expectations, like finding a
soulmate with looks, money, brains and heart, as well
as a carefree attitude to spending, are the bane of
our lives.

THINKING YOU HAVE FOUND HIM

First you will be in love with him (see earlier), with
any luck not too passionately. Passion will only blind
you to unhappy tendencies and the way his parents
have turned out. You will have noticed and documented

some shortcomings, had arguments you have resolved, recognised problems that probably won't go away and decided that whatever he may have done in the past, you can live with it.

You will have noticed that you want more or less the same sort of future, place a huge value on more or less the same things and laugh at the same things. You will have a big chunk of background in common; his points of reference will be familiar. I'm not advocating incest. But I don't think you can underestimate the tribal nature of most successful unions. Not that I married within the tribe. I did not. And how long have your father and I been together? I steeled myself, mind you.

YOUR FATHER

I walked down the aisle telling myself I could get divorced any time I wanted and on the second day of our honeymoon I tried to run away. I failed in this only because the honeymoon was on an island and the boat to the mainland came once a week. It wasn't that I didn't love your father. What panicked me was the folly I saw only too well in marrying the first man who'd asked me and whose family I had never seen. He was OK. He was twenty-seven and my family had already curled their lips at him. But I was nineteen. And we argued about everything, as we still do.

Oddly, despite being born twelve thousand miles apart, we had an astonishing amount in common: similar family structures, Catholicism, no telly, that kind of thing. We were both second born, both in journalism and we made each other laugh, mostly in despair.

We were opposites in some ways. He favoured the black side, I favoured the bright. He was fanatically neat, I was a slob. He had a very big head, I had a very small one. I loved change, he hated it. We didn't have the same politics and when we came back to England married, I loathed his friends.

Who can say why it worked, other than that possible sources of friction turned out to be helpful complements and I've never been bored. Naturally we loathe each other from time to time but the perfect partner is one you can loathe and learn to like again. Naturally there are times when we can't imagine living together a minute longer but the minute passes. Then we can't imagine living apart.

I can't say your father and I were wise in our choice. We were just lucky and we are both stickers. After we had you, we both wanted family life to work. With any luck we will remain lucky. With any luck it will continue to work, but it's a mad husband or wife who imagines it will just because it always has. If he starts buying only own brand products at Tesco's, I'm out of here.

How aggressive should you be in finding a husband

If you see someone you think looks half good, go after him and pin him down until you find out how good he is. The only thing to stop you should be his wife. Girlfriends should only stand in the way if they are yours. Don't be embarrassed if he rejects you. If he's the kind of man to reject you he'd have made a lousy husband. Check out that he wants what you want, make sure he kind of likes you, then go go go. That's if you want a husband. Many women get by very happily without one.

Marriage or not

I don't care, frankly.

Living together, view nothing

I used to think there was probably nothing wrong with cohabiting, view nothing but that was because I never did it. When I interviewed a whole lot of men about why the nation's sex lives are grinding to a halt, I changed my mind.

Many had lived together as a couple with girls early in their love lives, knowing that the relationships would end owing to everyone's all-round inexperience and youth. A hundred years ago, they might have married because you married locally then and the choice wasn't huge. Your first choice was probably your only choice.

No one much marries young these days in case they appear to be marrying in haste. So all these possibly perfect relationships ended, and the men were left feeling betrayed and bereft. It was like a divorce and it scarred them for ever. Now my advice is only to move in with someone you think you might marry if you are the marrying kind.

Seen one, seen them all

Obviously you lust after heaps of people and obviously you can fall in love with a lust object if you want to. You can also get to love a lot of men if you have the time and energy to compromise and they hang around long enough. There's no such thing as the perfect partner. What can be perfect is the partnership. All partners come with baggage. You have to decide how much effort you're prepared to put into shuffling your personal furniture about in order to accommodate his.

WHAT EVERYONE ELSE THINKS

Don't ask your father and me for our opinion. We won't have to live with him and we will never think anyone is good enough for you anyway.

Rule: If his baggage includes anything pink and fluffy, forget it.

How to get married

If, when and how you marry is entirely a matter for you. You will, however, be faced with moments of agonising choice. Here are some of them:

Precautions
prenuptial agreement/tacit understanding/we just love each other
Cultural experience
run away/stay home
Tact
involve families/do it yourself
Location
church/register office/wacky alternative
Minister
priest/celebrant/thoughtful person you met at yoga
Style
informal/formal/over the top
Guests
just the two of you/family only/friends only/close friends and immediate family only/everyone except the people you forget who will turn up at the church to look offended

When
morning/noon/night/morning, noon and night
Outfit
my dress/big white dress/simple off-white dress/suit/
bikini and lei
Transport
big cars/horse-drawn carriages/the Ford Escort/walk
Reception
marquee/hotel/restaurant/home/somewhere even
wackier
Greeting
reception line/name tags/awkward mêlée
Repast
finger food/buffet/sit-down three-course
Temperature of repast
hot/cold/hot cold
Taste of repast
prawn cocktail/no prawn cocktail
Cake
chocolate cake/fruit cake/something healthy
Your father
speeches/embarrassed silence/speeches followed by
embarrassed silence
Booze
free bar/limited bar/everyone goes home early
Merriment
dancing/no dancing
Sex
honeymoon/have one later/work is more important

These are the basics. I would never presume to
advise you.

Rule: *If you are marrying someone whose family is wildly different from ours I will still sing at the reception.*

MARRIED
LIFE

HOMECRAFT

In choosing a husband, follow my example and take a tidy man. This won't do if he is also violent since a violently tidy man will beat you if he thinks the place is in a mess. No. Marry a man who instinctively reaches for a broom at the end of a difficult day in the kitchen, who, without even thinking, washes up when he sees dirty dishes, gives the surfaces a good mop down, and who knows how to care for his own clothes.

Unless of course you are interested in homecraft yourself. Maybe you are. You have shown no signs of it in this particular home though baking has interested all of you in moments of insecurity and boredom.

TEST THE WATER

Halfway through our courtship when your father wanted to marry me and I was coming round to his way of thinking, I threw a massive tantrum. I said I could never marry since I could never be a housewife. Housewifery was as carbon monoxide to me and to have it forced upon me would ensure my ruin, I said. Maybe I fainted.

Your father said why was I making a fuss. He would never have expected me to be a housewife when it was plain I was a natural sloven. We would share the domestic duties. And he has been as good as his word. I could never have stayed married had he not.

DIVISION OF LABOUR

It was simple in your grandmother's day. She ran the house. The days when your grandfather picked up a tea towel, made a salad or prepared Sunday breakfast were red-letter days. It would have been her suffering that alerted me. She had no choice. She didn't go out to work so housework was her job and she did it with a funny, desperate look on her face.

Maybe it will be like this for you but it probably won't because most families these days need two incomes and you will have to work to earn money. Maybe you or your husband will work from home. Whatever, get the ground rules in place from the beginning. We're looking at a little prioritising here. Possibly lists and rotas. No one should get lumbered with the lot. Decide what's important and how it can be managed fairly.

In the case of your father and me, the division of labour was the most natural thing in the world and we have never argued about it though he has grumbled on many occasions about mess and lack of order. He says he doesn't clean because he likes it, only because he doesn't like the place not to be clean and I have decided to believe him although the peaceful look on his face when he's up to his elbows in suds is not one I recognise from my mother.

We pay someone to clean once a week and iron once a week. I tidy a bit; he does additional scrubbing, sweeping and mopping. We share the shopping, I do the cooking, he does the clearing up, I do the chauffering and clothe, nurse and see to the emotional and physical wellbeing of the children although he will chip in if anyone will listen. This works for us and always has but your father is the model of a husband in this respect.

ADVICE

Anything you need to know about ironing, you should get from him. He will also advise on washing powders, dishwasher salt (very important, he says), cleaning agents and sewing. I don't know if he is especially good at sewing but he gives it his all where I give it my nothing. By sewing, I don't mean dresses, I mean holes and buttons.

KNITTING

I can knit, however. You can all knit but none of us does any more and I fear knitting may soon vanish from the family line. This will be tragic. Your paternal grandmother was an inspired knitter.

I have knitted two famous garments. The first was a tiny yellow cardigan for my first baby which included a provision for a hunchback; the second was an immaculate royal blue school jumper which was worn once then thrown into the wash by your father where it shrunk. This was so painful I am not prepared to tell you any more about knitting unless you ask.

Your father's washing skills are not as finely honed as his cleaning skills. I am quite good at washing since I follow the principle of separating the load, which is a scientific one and widely abused.

THE WASHING

Remember that dear little jumper and always divide your load into whites, light coloureds, coloureds that could run and delicates that could shrink. Light coloureds can go in with the whites, coloureds that run should be on their own and delicates should be done by hand, in this case your father's to pay him back for his carelessness with my knitting. That is all you need to know about washing. If something gets discoloured, put it into a bucket of Napisan.

STAINS

Get stain-removing stuff. Put salt, tonic water or white wine on to red wine as soon as it is spilt. One or other of them works. I've forgotten which one.

COOKING

As far as I am concerned the art of homecraft is making a house into a home through cooking smells. Not all smells are acceptable though this is a cultural matter. In my culture, the smell of cakes baking, onions browning and meat roasting are to be valued above all others. Should you become vegetarian, forget the nut roast. It's not the same at all. Borrow some beef or lamb dripping from me and have it cook away in the oven just so that your children will be familiar with it.

It is of course the association of the smell that counts as you will know from Proust and your grandmother's house on Saturdays when she bakes and Sundays when she roasts. What the smells mean is that someone warm and loving is tending the hearth and that you will not only be safe and comfortable there, you will be fed something edible if you hang around long enough.

That's why you should cook. No matter how busy you are, even if you end up with sixteen children and a job running the country, cook so your children will remember the cosiness of their childhoods and pass it on to their children.

Here is a recipe for a sponge cake which takes no time at all to make and smells like mother's love. Just remember three. You want 3 ozs of sugar which you will beat into three eggs until the mixture is gold and doubled in quantity – three minutes roughly. Then fold in 3 ozs of plain flour sifted with some baking powder. A dollop. Fold it in, in three batches, with a light wrist. Tip into two greased and papered tins and cook at Mk 6 for 15 minutes. When cool, wedge together with fresh cream and raspberry jam or passionfruit pulp and your children will look at it and say, 'I don't like sponge cake.'

Rule: *Housework is only more important than having a laugh when there is mould in the fridge.*

How to buy a house and live in it happily

Buying a house is a major landmark in the test of time (see The Perfect Partner). It is during the purchase of a house that early signs of subsidence can appear in a marriage and you will have to resort to costly underpinning. Costly underpinning and subsidence will mean nothing to you but you should familiarise yourselves with the terms as they crop up repeatedly in domestic life especially one that involves as many moves as ours.

Subsidence

Subsidence is when the earth moves and your house starts to fall down. Before you can borrow any money to buy a house, the building society or bank will send round a surveyor whose job is to find some signs of it so they can turn down your application and feel smug about it.

More often than not, the surveyor will not find any

signs of it but he will find signs of collapsed drains, rotten roofs, faulty timbers, decrepit windows and beetle infestation and he will write about them all in a report which will make your partner freeze. This is a testing moment.

I am speaking of my husband here. I've only experienced the one so you may as well know what can happen if you hitch yourself to a man in your father's image. I'm not saying you will. I'm saying you might, so let me alert you.

Your husband will freeze when he sees this report and he will say only a fool would want to buy anything on the strength of it. You should say, 'I am that fool.' If the bank agrees to the purchase despite all the flaws it has found and you are passionate about the house, not to buy it is demented. You will already have looked at every other possible house in a two-hundred-mile radius, he will have found something wrong with every one of them and you will be ill at the thought of losing this one.

UNDERPINNING

Underpinning is how you prop up a house which is in danger of collapse. You can say to your husband, 'Have you never heard of underpinning?' but it won't help because a house which requires underpinning will not be regarded by the bank or moneylender as a good investment so it won't be an option for you. On the other hand underpinning may be required in your marriage at this juncture because large differences in your opinions may have appeared over where you should spend the next bit of your future and gaps of this sort are signs of subsidence. Definitely.

Standing firm has always been my response. 'Have you never heard of builders, new tiles, treated timbers and poison?' you can say. It's astonishing how things which sound so grim in a surveyor's report can turn out to be as nothing when viewed by a great builder. My life is littered with great builders. I have an almost mystic rapport with them and as a result have learnt much about the construction industry. That's why I can sound so confident.

MONEY

Before you even start looking for a house you must look at your money situation. I have done this so often I could be a mortgage broker. I understand as much as any domestic user of it needs to know about borrowing and lending and rolling over as well as comparing terms and penalty clauses.

Unless you marry a rich man, and why would you when I have taught you to disregard the importance of money, you will probably have to borrow. The chances are you will have saved nothing, yet you will be paying enough rent to support a pretty hefty mortgage. This won't be the case if interest rates are through the roof but you will be able to do that sum for yourself when the time comes.

You will usually need at least five per cent of the purchase price as a deposit. You can get this by hook or by crook. Hook is better (see Honesty). Your husband will say, 'We will have to do without all unnecessary items so we can save it. That's it for milk.' You may inform him that no such hardship need prevail. You can borrow the deposit as well. Borrowing is a terribly good way to raise money I have always found. The bummer is paying it back with whacking great chunks of interest on top but there, what's a bummer or two in house purchase?

Banks will normally give you two and a half times your combined incomes, or three times a single income and you should borrow as much as you can so you can afford the best house possible. This makes monetary sense. Even if property prices don't escalate in the leaps and bounds you had hoped, what you owe will be steadily reducing if you opt for a repayment mortgage which I would in your shoes.

Finding the best house possible can be a long and painful process during which you might have to hit each other in loft conversions and built-in wardrobes. It's not that you won't both want the same thing in principle; it's interpreting the principle as well as words like potential. Potential is something you can see that he can't. Your father calls this blindness being realistic.

CAVEAT EMPTOR – MY EXPERIENCE

We bought our Australian house at an auction on the very day property prices were on the verge of plummeting from an all-time high. It was never the ideal house but we were both sick of looking and I told your father we would get it for a great price, given the market and so on. He was worried about one or two things – like its humble appearance from the road – but I told him about the potential of the huge garden with a creek running through it and how we could fit a tennis court on to it.

According to the information provided by the agent, there were no hidden nightmares, so we went to the auction, had our bid forced up by several thousand dollars because we were too green to understand what was happening and came home triumphant. It wasn't until the first heavy rain that we discovered the creek flooded and the downstairs room leaked so badly it formed an indoor pool three feet deep.

Hey! I said brightly to your father but he didn't believe me. We fixed the problems in the end for a small fortune which we never recovered but we were happy there. When we sold the place and I wandered about it when it was empty, I could still hear the joyful peals of girlish laughter. It is a memory. Who needs a life full of memories without incident? That's what caveat emptor means. If you buy it and it's rubbish, provided it is what it says it is, to whit: a house you can live in, it's your own stupid fault if it goes wrong and your husband will only have you to blame.

Areas of dissent

Before you start looking you should agree on where you want to live, what you want to live in, how much you are going to spend and whether or not no proper bathroom will be a problem. It is odd how you can agree so much in principle but be so far apart in practice. It may help to reduce the testing moments if just one partner looks at properties and the other one looks at the short list.

So watch out

Eventually you will find a house which will have many flaws but none which can't be fixed for a sum that you will be able to afford before very long. You tell your husband that the marriage is over unless he buys it.

The chances are this will be the one house you've seen which has everything he ever said he wanted for the price.

Be prepared to be disappointed anyway. You can lose the house of your dreams for plenty of reasons other than your husband hating it. He will show himself to be the man he is by how he reacts to this tragedy.

A TRAGEDY FROM MY OWN LIFE

I once found the perfect house advertised in a newspaper by a man whose wife had recently died in it. We had to sell our own house but we had buyers so I felt confident. I was thrilled the widower wanted to sell to us because the price was rock bottom, there was a rose garden and there were many people wanting to buy it hovering like vultures in the drive. I kept going round there and listening to him tell me about his wife. Once he pinched my bum. I had booked the removalists, we were going to exchange and complete (see below) in the one day and then Lord and Lady blinking whatever they were called, pulled out of our purchase and everything fell into a screaming heap. I fell into screaming heap. It would have been the dead wife cursing me. Furious about my bum.

EXCHANGING AND COMPLETING

This can mean finding a more amenable husband and ending your marriage but in house purchasing terms it doesn't. It describes the two sections of the purchase. You pay your deposit and exchange contracts and then you arrange a day to complete the sale, usually a month later. Your solicitor will explain it. In marital terms it's the bit when you get to hate each other because there is a change in the offing and one of you will be coping with it much worse than the other.

Moving in

There's nothing I can tell you about moving in that will help. Get quotes from lots of firms. Don't go for the cheapest and don't start unloading yourself when the removalists say how bad their backs are. Your job is to stay cheerful because this is the house you wanted and already you can see five very good reasons why your husband might have been right.

Renovations

Improving the property may or may not improve your relationship. You might get a big buzz out of doing it up together. You may spend the entire period barely speaking. Taste is such a tricky little thing. I have always improved our properties with the help of many specialist workers and your father has always been extremely generous in allowing my taste to prevail. I tell him it's only because he has none but we both agree this is just me being unpleasant.

What you end up with

Unless you are very rich or obsessive or childless, you will end up with a permanently half-decorated house. This is called the family home. It takes ages and costs

a mint to get a place the way you like it and you will
no sooner have finished the last bit than the first bit
will need attention all over again. Even when you have
finished the last bit, there will always be a room with
funny light fittings or no light fittings. But this is fine.
You stop noticing within weeks and after a while your
husband says he likes things just the way they are.

Rule: Do not form romantic attachments to trades people.
Someone I knew had an affair with the carpenter and
produced many terrible symptoms which turned out after
exhaustive tests to be not splinters but guilt.

In-laws

M aybe you are too young to know about
mother-in-law jokes. They always used to begin
'My mother-in-law is so . . .' and usually she was fat
or ugly. I don't think people make them now because
mothers-in-law are so young and fit they can form
themselves into terrorist gangs to torch the pubs and
halls where the jokes are made and then go out for a
night of topless dancing.

I'm speaking of myself. I am practically a mother-
in-law since one of you is joined to a significant other
by everything except holy matrimony. Your father likes
to call him his son out-law but as jokes go, I prefer
ones starting my mother-in-law is so ugly. It's just your
father dealing with the awkwardness of current social
structures in his music hall way.

Marriage mightn't be the go any more but the
relationship between connecting families is just as
dodgy. There's a rich vein of bitterness in the whole
in-law set-up, based on resentment that a loved one
has tied herself to anyone so grotty and you might as
well know that I am no different even if I am very fond
of our granddaughter's father. Who could ever be good

enough for you? Who will ever treat you in the manner to which you have become accustomed which is the only manner for me?

Marriage cojoins families that are poles apart even when you marry the boy next door. You start off looking for faults and everyone battles uphill from there. This can improve with time. Familiarity will breed if not affection, at least acceptance, but in the case of your father, affection as well.

YOUR FATHER AS AN IN-LAW

It wasn't easy for him to meet my family or vice versa, as he arrived wearing a cream jacket, a smile from a toothpaste advertisement and doing jokes. My two previous boyfriends had been a junkie and a man with one leg who had made a point of having only one leg, so the family thought, 'Now she brings us a man who wants us to like him.' They hate people who want them to like them. Charm equals creep in my family. This was unlucky when charm was what your father did. Everyone except your grandfather went 'Oh no' when he proposed to me but he was around for so long they eventually got to see his good points and now he is as a son and brother to them all and knows all the songs. This happens. This is what you hope will happen in your case.

WHAT YOU CAN EXPECT

I can't imagine anyone not being completely thrilled to have you as one of them. But there's this funny thing between daughters and mothers-in-law and he is called her son. Mothers of sons always say, 'If you have a daughter you have her for life, you have a son till he takes a wife.' It's true really. A man can usually only manage one dominating woman in his life at a time and it's a sensible man who makes that woman the one he is living with.

How well you get along with your mother-in-law is entirely dependent on your husband. If he loves and respects his mother above everyone, would never dream of offending her and his name is Oedipus, you are in for a rocky old time. You'll be expected to be at her place for lunch every Sunday, every Christmas and other holy days, and he will drop everything at a moment's notice to be by her side. Ultimatums will have to be delivered because I will want you at our place some Sundays and some Christmases and possibly even holy days and it might even be better if you force an irretrievable alienation for his own good. I'm just thinking aloud.

What you need is a man who has separated emotionally from his mother, who has an easy, friendly relationship with her and who isn't frightened to say, 'Can we make that next week and not this minute?' unless of course her house is on fire, in which case he should make it quite clear that your guest room is for temporary use only.

Probably, if you continue to like your husband and his family haven't been completely beastly to him, you will get to like them and to have a good laugh with his mother. My mother-in-law, I'm sorry to say, is so dead that I no longer have a relationship with her. But I liked her a lot, I like your father's brothers a lot and I have become especially fond of his brother's wife. We have a bond which is unique and precious and provides constant reassurance about the gene pool.

WHY HUSBANDS TURN OUT LIKE THAT

Whether he likes it, fights it or not, your husband has inherited his parents' genes and so he will grow old and be just like one or other or a combination of both of them. This means you will end up sleeping with his mother or his father. The only consolation is that he is sleeping with your mother or your father.

AREAS OF DISCORD

You are most likely to fall out with your in-laws over the children and your husband's health. Your child-raising methods will almost certainly not be theirs and you will have to explain this to your children before or after they go to stay with them. Then the children will tell their grandparents what you have said and there will be frosty silences all round until your husband has a quiet word with you on the way home and you hit him. Then his mother will complain about his poor health and you will tell her if she's that bothered she can have him back so he has to have a quiet word with her and she says, 'I knew there'd be trouble the minute I clapped eyes on her.'

THEY ARE HIS FAMILY AFTER ALL – DON'T FORCE HIM TO CHOOSE

Still, they are his family which makes them your family. And sooner or later, that is how you come to see them. You will throw their bad points at your husband whenever it suits you and he will throw your family's bad points back at you since bad points provide excellent ammunition for sneaky counter-attacks.

The silliest thing you can do is force him to choose between you and them and the silliest thing he can do is allow the choice to crop up. Don't marry a silly man, for God's sake.

Rule: I will make any man you bring into the house welcome but don't expect your father to talk to him about football.

WHEN AND HOW TO SAVE
YOUR MARRIAGE

M ost marriages are worth saving despite the general view that one in every two or three are duds. You may not have always thought so from listening to your father and me discussing cleanliness but it is true. What's the point in swapping one set of difficult circumstances for another set when it deprives children of living with two parents they love? And look at the divorcees we know – how many are much, much happier?

You get out quick smart when your physical or mental health, or the physical and mental health of the children is in mortal peril. But you grin and bear it if it's passing peril. Maybe grin is overstating the case. You put up with it. Passing peril is everyday life and everyday life is sometimes bad, sometimes good but usually kind of OK. There's nothing wrong with exposing children to passing peril.

PERIL – MORTAL

Don't marry a drunk or a man who hits. Always leave
a violent husband. I will come and get you. Drinking is
less cut and dried. Of course, since the drunk is always
half cut and never dried out. At its worst booze destroys
normal family life. I should know because I grew up
with it and we only managed normal life because your
grandmother was heroic.

What you hope is that the drunk will tackle his
problem and save the day but mostly he won't until
you kick him out. He will keep on promising and trying.
Only you will know how much you can stand. It will be
when I've yelled myself hoarse although it will be none
of my business.

Should you have to end your marriage, do so
knowing you have tried your hardest and that coping
on your own is infinitely preferable to coping with a
useless husband. This will be liberating and uplifting
and we will all be there to cheer you on.

PERILS – PASSING

The peril which passes includes feeling unhappy,
stressed, exhausted, tempted by other men, taken for
granted and sick to death of your husband's wretched
slurping. You deal with it how you like. I like to scream
then get a migraine which breaks the tension because
your father then says how many headaches have I had
this week and am I sure I don't have a brain tumour.
Why something bugs you one day and not another is a
mystery to me. Just know it happens.

Outgrowing

Almost certainly you will wake up one morning and notice that the person you agreed to stay with till death parted you no longer exists. It's no reason for stomping off. What kind of people would you be if you didn't change? Even dead people change. What did you think? That you wouldn't? This change is a reason for having a life beyond your marriage (see Hobbies later).

The biggest mistake you can make is to imagine one person can and must satisfy your every physical, emotional, financial, intellectual, spiritual, professional and culinary need. How could he? He need only be a partner in an arrangement which will probably involve the raising of children in reasonably happy and comfortable circumstances and all you need from him is affection, respect and help which is more than you will get if you are a single parent and lonely.

Childless perils

The severity of perils is really neither here nor there if you don't have children. You can please yourself about leaving since you only have each other to hurt. But even then, all the above still applies. I would counsel patience, especially when you have already put so much effort into being accommodating. It's amazing what changes if you hang on. Hair grows, laughs change, tempers improve, bridgework can eradicate slurping.

Your father and i

We are always going off each other. He thinks I am an
arrogant know-all cow and I think he is a grumbling,
deaf lunatic. This goes on for a bit then it stops.
While we are disliking each other he will continue to
telephone from work once or twice a day and we will
continue to have a drink together in the evenings. This
is habit. Our affection has become a habit. Perhaps this
is sad but I take comfort from it.

How close it's come for us

Your father once marched out on your grandmother and
me when we were in Paris. We had gone there just after
the birth of our first baby. Your grandmother, who had
come to London for the birth, was about to go back to
Australia so it was supposed to be a treat but I had an
infected bottom from too many stitches. He left because
I said I wouldn't walk to the Tuileries Gardens or have
a big meal for lunch. He may remember this differently,
but what does it matter?

This was obviously a perilous time. Not long after,
I left home in my socks because we had fallen out over
the laundry man who was sacked after your father
complained about him. I stayed out all night, sleeping
on a friend's sofa. Then I went home.

From this you can deduce that some times are more
perilous than others. House-moving is one. Having
babies is another. Money shortage is another.

OTHER PEOPLE'S PERILS – LIKE SEX

The usual misery with sex is when the husband or wife
turns out to be having it with someone else. This you
will say is mental and physical torment and the ultimate
in lack of respect. But lots of adulterers are devoted
to their husbands and wives and have very decent
arrangements with them which are worth preserving.
So why are they bonking about, you will cry. Vanity
probably when they can slake their lust at home. Unless
of course they can't slake their lust at home owing to
the lustre having gone out of their sex lives, which can
happen.

WHOOPS – NO SEX

A husband and wife can go off each other owing to
fatigue, boredom, physical disgust or lack of effort and
this can be extremely hurtful or a relief depending on
the sex drives involved. If this happens to you and
you suspect it is driving your husband into the arms of
other women, you should get counselling. There are
all sorts of things you can do which come in brown
paper packages. Probably best not to involve me but if
you do get something in brown paper I would be very
interested to see it.

WHOOPS – WEIRD SEX

Maybe it's what's in the brown paper packaging
that puts you off your husband. If he is kinky and
makes unnatural demands on you, then of course
get out. Unless you like unnatural demands. Plenty

of very decent people are into bondage, leather and sex which requires equipment, but with the children in the next room wanting drinks of water and to go to the loo all night, how? Should your husband not be decent and should he inflict his awful tendencies on you – go.

BETRAYAL

Maybe your husband is having sex elsewhere with a woman he says he loves. Get shot of him at once or you definitely will go into a physical and mental decline. There's no point in letting him have the best of both worlds when you have only the worst of one. Order him out and change the locks. What must he be like? Everyone says true love can strike like this – out of the blue, wham! when you aren't expecting it – but I've always thought you had to be up for it in the first place. And you shouldn't be up for it if there are children at home and home is chugging along very nicely.

MONEY

Your father and I rarely row about money and I don't think I could stand it if we did. It's so . . . grimy. Having none is a joint problem. It's when only one person is to blame for having none that it gets nasty.

If it's a question of being broke with no real way out, then it's much better you face the problem together. If it's a question of one person spending far more than is fair, then separate accounts and standing orders from the spendthrift's account to cover his or her obligations has to be the answer. But this would be a band-aid thing. The spendthrift needs help. The sex counsellor may double up. It'd save a bob which would be handy under the circumstances.

You need to get your money arrangements agreed early in the piece though this isn't to say they can't change as your income and outgoings change. Your father and I began with separate accounts and now we have about ten joint accounts. It strikes me that if you have a little respect and a mutual need for a comfortable existence then only a worm would spend more than his or her fair share and since you wouldn't marry a worm, he will have gone round the bend and could need committing.

DISCIPLINE

I don't mean as in bondage. I mean as in children. This can be a bone of contention simply because you and your husband were brought up differently. And what you want is consistency. We have found consistency by doing it my way.

I have always done the technically unforgivable, which is to side with you against your father if I thought he was being irrational and mean. It has occasionally infuriated him beyond measure but he takes heart from the fact that he is completely adored by all of you and you don't care if he is irrational and mean.

What was I supposed to do anyway? Sit there like a Victorian dummy in the face of such provocation? He would do the same to me if I was sounding irrational and mean. I just don't sound irrational and mean. Right?

HOLIDAYS

Husbands and wives nearly always fall out on holiday because they have nothing better to do. Suddenly there is all this adrenaline which would normally be used up at work with nowhere to go, and here is all this stress related to a new place, strange beds, odd food, ridiculous currency and cars on the wrong side of the road, so tempers flare. The discord usually only lasts a few days and then the husband relaxes a bit. It's a lesson for life, really.

COMMUNICATE

I love that story about the man who was moving some of your stuff from a flat into storage. He was talking about the last job he had done. 'They were in a total mess, innit?' he said. 'She was sayin' one fing, he was sayin' anuvver. I held up my hands. I showed 'em. I said, "Right hand, left hand!"' He smashed his hands together. '"Communicate."' That's the sum of it. You have to thrash it out, whatever it is, however ugly it gets. You don't want to involve the children but if they hear bits of it, it won't kill them. They won't mind you fighting, so long as they see you making up. That's how it's been in our place. You will have learnt something from us, even if it's how not to run a family life.

Rule: Don't ask children for an opinion when arguing with their father. They might side with him.

MOTHERHOOD

How to have a baby

First, how much water should be present? It's not easy. Do you want to invest in a birthing pool, might you prefer your husband boiling kettles and sharpening his penknife or are you going to settle for your own being broken in hospital by a midwife who wants to get things moving?

It all gets terribly technical but the idea is not to obsess. I can't stomach women who obsess about childbirth. In the end it's a simple question of what is in there getting out and you want it to get out as painlessly and healthily as possible with no fuss. The role of water has always been crucial but now, what you do with it indicates the kind of start in life you want your child to have.

Birthing pools were not an option when I had babies but these days, the serene mother, who imagines she will be in control of her destiny, often chooses it so her baby can float into the world looking waterlogged. You might like that idea.

The home birth is increasingly popular for parents who have read many books about it and don't want their baby's first breath to involve disinfectant. This is very cosy with the father boiling kettles and so on. But for even the very slightly neurotic mother, hospital has better resuscitation facilities. Know yourself, know your birthing technique, that's my advice to you.

HOSPITAL IN MY EXPERIENCE

This is the only technique on which I can speak with authority since it's the only one I tried and I tried it three times using three different London teaching hospitals. The first birth was difficult, involving the smashing of my waters by a midwife who wouldn't allow me to steady myself on the bed head and a third degree tear which had to be stitched under general anaesthetic. The second was OK but, despite my telling the midwife that the birth was imminent, I was given pethidine and the baby arrived drugged to the eyeballs. The third was brilliant. I said the baby is coming, they said no it isn't, then they took another look and said yes it is. I said I didn't want any cutting and the midwife told the boy who thought he was delivering the baby that he should listen to the mother.

The baby was born smoothly, there were no stitches and the paediatrician on stand-by pronounced the baby a girl, pink and beautiful. By the time I had sauntered back to the ward, the baby had gone blue and was in intensive care. You can make of that what you will. I would have been in trouble had I involved any waters other than my own. But hospital isn't a barrel of laughs in the water department.

MORE WATER

Someone always gets up your nose giving the baby
water when you've asked them not to or a bottle
when you are trying like mad to make the breast more
inviting. This is infuriating because you are devoting
all your energy to making this baby yours. Otherwise,
hospital is a boon in this respect. Someone else is
cooking, you're not expected to answer the phone or
to live any life other than the one involving you and the
baby. Your husband may come in with many worries
about pasta and school runs but you are relatively
protected. At home, you are the wife and mother.
Unless you have someone to help, you will very shortly
feel knackered and put upon.

DOES IT HURT?

Only the way squeezing something the size of a melon
out of your vagina hurts. Because you know it will get
out eventually and that the pain isn't a deadly disease,
you can handle it.

DRUGS

If you want them, go for the lot. If you don't want them
spit and cry, 'Drugs, never!' Somewhere in the middle is
about right.

TO SCREAM OR NOT

It would offend me terribly to hear myself scream. This is because I consider myself hard and stoic in the face of pain. But lots of brave women yell and everyone thinks it's a big laugh. Many women curse their husbands. When I am giving birth I have forgotten what my husband had to do with it.

ME AND SCREAMING

After the third birth, a very young nurse with an uppitty expression dropped by my bed and said, 'You made enough noise yesterday.' I looked at her askance. I asked her which noise that would have been. She thought I was joking. She said the noise I'd made screaming the place down as the baby emerged. I said it wasn't me. She said of course it was me. I said it wasn't. She said it was. She asked what room I'd been in. I told her. She said then it was you. I told her to sod off. She put it down to post partum lying but had I not been in a post partum ecstasy I would have hit her (see rule on punching).

POST PARTUM

This means after you've given birth and it's the bit where you cry. I only cried once in hospital and that was after the first birth because I had to be in hospital for weeks and weeks with a tiny, sleepy baby who was still on the six o'clock feed when all the other babies were being winded after the ten o'clock and I'd had enough. The woman in the next bed was called Udder and her son was called Tits. They were Italian. She spelt her name Ada and Tits was short for something starting with Tits but I thought they were out of a Fellini film and were there to haunt me. Sylvester Stallone would have cried.

You are expected to cry a bit owing to your hormones being everywhere and your husband being such a prat. Also everyone expects you to get post natal depression. I never did but I know women who have and it is terrible. I will look after you should it strike you down.

HUSBANDS

On the other hand, I loved having him there. He's never been much use during the labour because he bores easily but for the birth itself, he is great at crying, 'Push.' And afterwards he's been brilliant on the phone telling everyone how it went. I don't think he'd be much cop with a penknife. I will be at your side if you want me for your births but if the father is to be there, the last person you need is your mother.

Rule: If you must scream, scream at someone. Look for the one who will give your baby water. You will know her by the irritating look on her face.

HOW TO BE THE MOTHER
OF ALL MOTHERS

Both you and your husband will want only happiness and fulfilment for your children but one of the first things you will discover about mothering is that it is different from fathering. You will discover this not long after the birth, in the middle of the night, when the baby cries.

Mothering, you will find, involves waking up and doing something about it. Fathering involves waking up and going back to sleep or waking up and saying, 'Does it want something?' The biological explanation for this is that women have breasts.

You can either refuse to buy it and give the father lots of kicks while yelling that it's his turn to change the nappy and he's a lazy git, or you can get up and see to the baby yourself. If you choose more times than not to get up because it's easier, this will set the tone for your mothering and you will find yourself largely responsible for the child's emotional welfare, education, physical health, music lessons and driving about.

ME AS A MOTHER

This is what has happened in our place. Your father is an excellent parent in that he cares passionately about you, will go to the ends of the earth to spare you pain and suffering and has always taken you on excellent outings to feed the ducks, but he has rarely remembered the names of your friends, known what subjects you are doing at school or spent more than a minute listening to stories from your troubled lives.

This isn't a complaint. He takes care of the car, the lawn mowing, the washing, the VAT returns, the washing up and taking rubbish to the tip. The distribution of labour in our house has suited me fine. I have loved every minute of being a mother. But there are some aspects of family life which require special consideration so I'll mention them and you can consider.

PETS

You buy pets so children will learn about mating, death, flea infestation and smells via the animal kingdom. Unless you are a huge pet lover yourself, forget it.

Children only want animals they can cuddle in moments of boredom or misery and they don't ever accept responsibility for scraping Whiskas off the kitchen floor and emptying the kitty litter. Nor will they change the goldfish water or buy extra pond stuff with their pocket money.

Owing to the rise of the roving psychopath, they will not be able to walk the dog until they are over six feet tall and weighing more than eleven stone, by which time a dog is the last thing in the animal kingdom which will be of immediate interest.

I say children. I mean you. Yet you have all taken pains to tell me how deprived you have been. Frankly I think two cats, ten rabbits and eight goldfish is enough for anyone.

CHILDCARE

If you pursue your careers once you have children, you will need childcare. There is no greater source of angst for the modern mother. It always seems to be the modern mother and not the modern father who has to fix it and the modern mother whose job must suffer if the arrangement falls down. This will be about breasts as well.

It is generally held that in an ideal world the role of childcarer should fall to the grandmother. Excuse me? The grandmother has already raised her own children and once round the block on that one is enough. She is there for emergencies if her own career allows it, babysitting and many happy holidays and visits.

Childcare means nannies, crèches or childminders and the choice you have will depend on how much you earn. None of them ever looks entirely normal on first viewing. When seeking childcare look first for signs of potential violence and abnormalities of speech. You will not want your children speaking with strange accents or using the language incorrectly.

Check that there will be affection – love is overdoing it – security, reliability, stimulation, proper food, hygiene, consistency and proper attention. You can do this by hiding when potential minders are with your child and seeing how they are. Never be frightened of changing an arrangement that gives you the creeps and never hang in there just because you don't have time to find a better alternative.

There is no need to worry that the childcarer will replace you in your child's affections unless of course you are absent so long that the child forgets what you look like. You need to make sure that the time you spend with your children is 'quality time', a modern term which means playing chess.

Your needs will change according to the age of the children. You think everything will improve once they are at school, but this only applies if you can do your job in school hours. Otherwise you need to make complicated provisions for after school hours and holidays. Working from home is one answer. It was the answer for me. Not only could I be there for you when you were home, I didn't have to mix with people and this is a boon beyond compare.

ME AND CHILDCARE

You will read a whole lot of palaver telling you that leaving your children to the care of anyone not involved in their conception will damage them irreparably and bring about social decay. Burn it. There are studies to prove anything, as I discovered when I wrote a guide for working mothers to reassure me when the first of you was a baby. The simple underlying truth seems to be that, provided you have good quality care appropriate to the needs of your child, the child looks happy and you are content, future delinquency will have nothing to do with you working.

I whipped you out of two situations which I hated and finally settled for help in the home because that's where I was working. This was the luxury of all luxuries but even so, it wasn't without its heart-attack moments. I had to sack the nanny who had entered in her diary, 'The baby was a little bitch today.' Served me right for reading the diary. Served her right for leaving it lying around when she might have guessed I put the happiness of my baby before her privacy.

CATERING

A good many husbands are now as keen on cooking as their wives and it is no reflection on their manhood that they spend longer than she does in the kitchen. The reason is simple. Cooking is the best and most creative of all the domestic chores and it's better to be good at that than ironing. This is my view anyway.

Catering, however, is not without its hardships. A mother must take into account the tastes of all family members which can on occasion reduce the number of dishes acceptable to all to one. This is a pain in the neck. Be firm about food faddism. Withdraw all food if you must until most family members come round to your way of thinking.

Do not overbuy. It takes a great deal of ingenuity but provides enormous satisfaction to use up everything in the fridge by the end of the week. Throwing out is not a happy solution for leftovers but, if it won't go into a cake or a soup and no one will touch it in a salad or on toast, let it go.

EXTRA CURRICULAR

The lot of extending the child so that it can reach its
full potential usually falls to the mother who must
arrange music, dancing, gym, tennis, riding, skating and
self-defence lessons according to the funds available,
the interest of the child, the availability of the classes
and the degree of frustration felt by the mother who
was never able to get classes in her own childhood.

You

You are all women of accomplishment because that's
what your father and I wanted to spend our money on.
Owing to my fear of boredom, I took huge pleasure in
giving you the wherewithal to entertain yourselves any
time any place. It helped that you were talented. You
can sing, you can play the piano, the violin, the cello,
the penny whistle, the guitar and the recorder. As my
father pointed out, I could play only the fool.

You can draw and paint. You can ride, play tennis
and dance but you can't do embroidery. In that I have
failed you. I don't know who has taken most pleasure
from your many accomplishments. Probably me and if
you have the money, the time and the energy I strongly
urge you to do the same for your children. They will
then be fully rounded which is the correct thing for the
modern child to be and has nothing to do with bra size.

CHAUFFERING

In the pursuit of these accomplishments, as well as
their social lives, you will spend many, many hours
in the car, trekking across England and connected
territories. It is very tiring and there are many bad
people on the road who see your face across a steering
wheel, recognise you as a very tired mother who has
spent too long in a church hall watching *pliés*, and who
will decide to ram you. These people are men with
retarded sexual development. You deal with them by
winding down the window and yelling, 'Got a penis
problem? Sorry, children. That man was very silly.' This
relieves neck ache.

LISTENING

Just as your children stop needing you to drive them so
many places, they require you to listen to them which
takes up even more energy and concentration. Or they
won't want to speak to you which also requires a great
deal of energy and concentration because you must
get them to open up or watch them shrivel before your
very eyes.

You want them to talk about their friends, their
work, their hopes, their fears, their spots, their hair,
their dreams and so on. Usually they will only speak to
you when it suits them and this will be when you are
on the phone, in the bath or about to go to sleep. Take
vitamin B6 for brain power.

SICK CHILDREN

A nanny comes into her own when the children are sick because the child can stay in her own bed and you can still go to work. But once the children are at school, you have usually finished with the nanny. When the children are sick you must take time off work to care for them even though you have meetings booked with heads of state. Maybe the father can take time off work more easily but in my experience this is unheard of and 'easily' doesn't count.

The first thing you must do is test for genuine sickness. This can involve the thermometer – 'If you don't have a temperature you can go to school'; vomiting – 'If you're not sick again within the next hour I think you'll be all right'; and rashes – 'Look, it's faded.' But if the child is truly ill, forget it. Cancel everything, become a nurse and enjoy it, which you can provided the symptoms aren't too worrying. You can watch lots of lovely TV together. In the event of worrying symptoms, forget work altogether. The child should always come first and the labour market needs to acknowledge and accommodate this.

HOW TO BE IN TWO PLACES
AT THE SAME TIME

Time management has always been the secret of successful mothering and never more so when successful mothering must be combined with successful money-earning. We still don't have a mobile phone but I can see how they would be invaluable for letting everyone know where you are and how long you will be. Without one, you need watertight arrangements for children being at a piano lesson and not at someone's house for tea and for there being food for supper as opposed to 'I know, McDonalds' again.'

Sometimes if you have more than two children you will be required to be in three places at the same time. You can do this by making clever and timely appearances and plotting your route through back streets to avoid traffic jams. There have been times in my life when I have had three children at three different schools in three different parts of London and all of them have had something on. The important thing is to be there for the bit that counts or at least to give the impression you have been. 'Shame Mary was so ugly – poor little Jesus' is always a good observation.

Making the most of the time available is essential. Prepare yourself en route, arrive focused, note remarks, performances, pictures on the wall and where your child is standing.

Sometimes you will have to explain to one or other child that you just can't be there but this is rarely acceptable – a present helps.

BRIBES

Presents are good. There are times when what you have to do will be completely offensive to your child – like going out when they want you to stay in. Then you must bribe them because there is no reason why they can't be made a little happier when you are going off to be happy.

EVERYTHING ELSE

There is so much more. Ask me when the time comes.

Rule: Never let their father cut your children's hair. He will do it for precision rather than style and they will look like escapees from the armed forces.

Rules and applying them

I have already touched on the difficulty of having two parents wanting to lay down the law in day to day child-raising. Especially two with different takes on right and wrong. You would think that a child raised under such conditions would grow up with massive fractures down the middle of its psyche from being torn asunder. But this doesn't seem to have happened in your case. I like to think that your father's and my different perspectives have given you a balanced outlook.

I could be wrong. If you think I am, you will avoid the mistake by marrying a man who is so in tune with you that you are as one on everything. Yuk!

Your own childhood – an example

Your father likes his possessions to be where he left them, in the condition that he left them, and he isn't all that keen to share. This would be because he fears no one will care for them as he does. Boy does he care for them! He is scarred in regard to possessions and this is something we should take into account at all times.

Take something of his – his scissors in particular – fail to return them, and he will carry on as if you had killed the cat. None of you would ever kill the cat.

When you respond in a careless fashion to his irritation, he becomes even more enraged and eventually I will say, 'Hang on. How bad is it? She hasn't killed the cat.' And your father will express the view that I am undermining his authority and the reason you are so selfish is because I have encouraged it. Maybe he has a point. But I can't get into that missing scissors thing.

I hate only one or two things: deceit and murder in all their forms, and I despise only a few other things including wanton destruction and being very rude indeed. I will make a big fuss about any of these but to make a big fuss over something minor which can be explained and regretted in a civilised way is to undermine the big fuss when it is needed.

Your father is also opposed to lying and theft, but mainly as they pertain to his possessions and he is also opposed to children being very rude indeed. He sometimes says you are more often very rude indeed to him than you are to me because no one respects him as father of the house and I tell him dead right. Father of the house is no more significant than mother of the house and he must make his own way with regard to respect.

Sometimes when he feels I have undermined his authority, I say to him, 'This is teenage anger and what would you rather have, an angry child or one into self-mutilation?' This bucks him up.

Work it out for yourselves

Since I am not one hundred per cent sure that I have
behaved impeccably as a mother when it comes to
accommodating the interests of your father in our joint
child-raising, I think I will have to advise you to work it
out for yourself. It's a juggling act. However, under no
circumstances should you tell your children to wait until
their father gets home. And under no circumstances
should you give the impression of ganging up.

A united front is all very well but a united front
should contain one silent partner. There is nothing
more horrible for a child than to hear two loud voices
haranguing in unison. It makes them feel trapped
and overwhelmed. You know this, naturally. I'm just
reminding you.

Rules

Enforcing rules is exhausting, so have as few as
possible. Then stick to the ones you've made or your
children will think you are weak as water and never
take you seriously again. The rules will change with age,
obviously. The older the children get, the more likely
you are to negotiate. But you should never turn your
back on a rule that has been broken even if it is in the
middle of the night and you are ill from exhaustion.

Punishment

This will depend on how angry you are at the time.
Lose your temper badly and the punishment will almost
certainly involve some kind of physical response.

Children who are up to your shoulder will get a whack to the bottom. Children who are head high will get a clip round the ear. This will normally be owing to very-rude-indeedness.

If your child is articulate and politically aware as you all are, they will threaten you with the police or the NSPCC and this will make you angrier because you will know you have raised little smart alecs and it was because they were being smart alecs and offensive that you lost it in the first place. Already you will feel silly and possibly regretful that you are out of control, so you will calm down.

The big, big joy about a quick slap is that it relieves the tension on all sides. The child will already know she has overstepped the mark and will be expecting something horrible to happen. She will almost be willing something horrible to happen. A hit might be undignified and outrageous but it also ends the matter.

In lesser circumstances, and they are far more usual, you still must respond to broken rules and the usual thing is to send a child who is aged under four to sit on the stair, over four to her room and then possibly to withhold some treat or other. Gating applies once the child is old enough to have regular outings that matter. I was never much good at withholding treats. You might be firmer.

CODE

A lot of trouble can be avoided if you establish a code early on which says you are pushing your luck. In public I have always favoured the very firm grip on the bicep as I have led you to a quiet corner to remonstrate. I've always thought this was subtle and that I displayed

positively nothing but calm. You say my lips are always scrunched up and my eyes bulging. I can't argue.
The bicep grip remains very effective with or without the lips.

You should also develop eyeballing which is to give a short, loaded look which says try that once more and I will have you by the bicep before you can say NSPCC.

To be honest, I never needed to think very hard about discipline. You were very well behaved as small children and very easy to distract. Always distract before you confront. It's so much nicer. As you have grown older, arguing very loudly, followed by clever bartering, has resolved most things. With any luck, your children will be as lovely as mine and your husband as sensible.

Rule: Don't offer too many choices. They just confuse the issue. You know what's acceptable. Offer it or nothing.

Avoiding embarrassment
at school

The role of the parent at school is to look normal. This can be achieved as follows:

1. Choosing the right one.
This will be one whose idea of a good education coincides with your own, otherwise you will always be down there complaining and your child won't see any reason to go. Sending your child to the school you went to only works if you are remembered fondly as a good and able student. Do not delude yourself or have fonder memories than is helpful.

2. Behaving sensibly at parent/teacher interviews.
The object of these is to persuade the teachers that your child is a genius and their job is simply to unlock the door. Do not take your husband if, like mine, he spends the allotted five minutes reminiscing about his own school days and getting the teacher's name wrong.

3. Not wearing funny clothes.

You will recall two incidents involving me and a very short skirt and me with pink and purple hair. The first caused one of you to rush at me and wrap my coat tightly about me, all the while yelling, 'Every other mother is wearing floral to the knee.' The second caused another of you to walk past me in the playground as if I was somebody else's mother and to burst into tears when I ran after you. What constitutes funny will depend on your child and the school but know that children, even yourselves, are notoriously conservative when it comes to mothers and you must dress like every other one, even if this means shoving on an Alice band.

4. Never arriving at school drunk.

The smell of wine is bad on a mother's breath and you will almost certainly say something you will regret.

5. Not overreacting.

This has been a failing of mine. Whenever a child or teacher has done anything to cause you offence, instead of shrugging it off as one of life's challenges, I have gone bananas and dwelt on the slight for many days, plotting revenge and railing about the aggressor's unhinged prejudice. I don't think this has been altogether helpful, on reflection.

6. Don't go on about homework.

Your child will either do it or she won't. You doing it will be a dreadful embarrassment because you won't have been at the lesson where the teacher said under no circumstances refer to the caterpillar when a caterpillar is all you can draw and you have done an excellent one. Failure to do homework is the child's look-out and she will soon become conniving and scheming, or a swat, or somewhere in between. It will be her responsibility and saying so is excellent parenting as well as easier all round.

Rule: Always go to the nativity play even if your child isn't Mary or the angel. There is no finer drama constantly performed in the western world today. Ask about the casting though. There is such unfairness.

Teenagers: drugs and other forms of self-abuse

Since you still have half a leg in the teenage camp, you will recognise the dilemmas I am about to describe and possibly decide to keep a diary which will be a primary source when you forget what it was like later.

The troubles

A diary will be helpful because it takes one or two goes at it for a mother to appreciate that the years from twelve to twenty-two are a period of relative insanity – both the child's and the parents' – and you survive them only by breathing. There will be many occasions during this patch when you will find you have stopped breathing, from fury, fear, outrage or hurt, and unless you resume you will die.

When this happens first time round, you put it down to deviant behaviour in the child and wonder how you have failed her. As time passes, her behaviour kind of lessens, and she becomes the charming, sensible, thoughtful person you'd hoped for. Then the second and third start but you are ready for them.

It's all about separation. The first child has to fight hardest to separate because the parents, in your case the mother, isn't prepared for it. She needs to stamp on her mother's fingers as her mother dangles off this metaphoric cliff. The teenage person must stamp so hard the mother lets go.

It's very painful, especially when the mother knows that fourteen or fifteen is too early to let go. Young people are so dreadfully into self-abuse and I mean that in the broadest sense of the term. It's how to protect them without stifling them. You do your best, but at what cost.

YOU AS TEENAGERS

The worst thing all of you have been is provocative. This has, on occasion, been so breathtaking that in order to exhale I have had to chase you – once up the street calling, 'Come back here. Never leave this house in a temper.'

All of you have wanted to go places where it has been illegal to go; all of you have wanted to stay out longer than I could stand; all of you have mixed with people I considered a rum lot. I have had to use my discretion and I used it so much that it became wafer thin.

The trouble is, there are so few places a fifteen-year-old can legitimately go for laughs. Friends' houses are only so interesting and friends' parents only so accommodating. How many parents want ten rowdy youths around every Saturday night?

You have all been amenable to negotiation and only rarely abused the privilege. I am grateful for that. But it has never stopped me lying awake at nights and imagining the worst. You will find yourself in the same position because I can't imagine it changing. You can trust your teenage child to the high heavens but you can't trust everyone else and it's exposure to everyone else in unprotected circumstances that is a parents' nightmare. According to you, I'm the strictest mother you know. All I can say is you don't know many mothers. I hope I've been as strict as I needed to be.

You were well off

Just be grateful you weren't raised by your grandmother. How well I remember the night I was taken out by a young reporter on the paper where I was a copy girl. We went out in his car and met friends and had a laugh. It was the usual night of drink and lechery and should have ended at a reasonable hour but on the way home we collided with another car at an intersection. Instead of being delivered to my door by midnight, I was delivered at two. Your grandmother was waiting with all the lights and her dressing gown on. What a terrible sight to behold. She attacked this poor boy. She was having none of any car crash. She implied all sorts of depravity and he could do no more than apologise. I had to go inside with a silly look on my face even though she told me to get it off.

I never did that to you. And she never did that to my younger sister either. It's the way of it.

TRUST

Trust is all very well but only a dopey mother is completely trusting. You reckon you don't have secrets from me but that is always after the event. It's a parent's job to anticipate the hazards of an event and steer the child clear of it. She can only ever do this successfully some of the time.

DRUGS

Who knows what the situation will be when your children are your age? Certainly you've all been offered drugs of one sort or another from the time you were about thirteen. There is positively nothing a parent can do to stop a child from trying them short of locking her in a room twenty-four hours a day or having her followed by a minder twenty-four hours a day and even then, can you trust the minder? You hope your children will have the sense to be aware of the dangers and the strength to acknowledge them. All drugs have risks, none more so than booze and cigarettes. They not only do your body in, they can do your head in. You tell that to your children and your children go, 'I know.' The only answer is eternal vigilance.

SUSPICION

You thought I was crazy the time I accused you of solvent abuse when you were only taking off your nail varnish but give me a break. There were mood swings, irrational behaviour and closed doors as well as a horrible chemical smell. What else was I to make of it?

SEX

You should talk to your children about sex from the day they eat their first egg. It oughtn't to be a source of embarrassment or difficulty. By their teenage years they should feel able to discuss it freely. If your position is judgemental and censorious, you've had it. You will be deemed not to understand.

One of you once asked me about masturbation and I replied truthfully that when I was that age, I'd never heard of it, let alone done it. I was under the influence of nuns who said it was a sin to touch your body. You took this to mean I thought it was gross which was a terrible misunderstanding.

To avoid something similar yourself, tell amusing stories from your own sex life. It wasn't something I felt comfortable with but you might. Should you have sons, you will need to know that teenage boys have wet dreams. Girls have dry dreams which is less awkward.

EVERYDAY LIFE

The best you can hope with your teenagers is that they will talk to you, occasionally listen to you and not mind being seen out with you from time to time. They will yell at you, say stuff you'd never have dreamed of saying to your mother, slam doors and hoard damp towels in their bedrooms.

They will leave coffee cups in the sitting room, endless glasses of water and possibly half-eaten bits of food by their bed, and they will nick your make-up and clothes. They will be surly when you are tired and irrational when you are trying to make them see sense. All of this is normal and a normal mother will occasionally do her nut but breathe on until the years pass.

They can at the same time be brilliant company. And there is nothing more heart-warming than to see your tiny children growing into smart, funny, charming grown-ups who know how to behave when they're out. You'll love it.

Rule: *Keep pregnancy testing kits on hand. There will always be emergencies.*

SURVIVAL

COPING MECHANISMS

Among a mother's many jobs is to cope in a crisis. This is to reassure the children that everything is under control and no one need panic. You have to do this whether you feel like it or not. A mask of indifference is one way of doing it but this can be confused with everyday indifference and sooner or later your children will remind you how callous you were.

I like to think I am quite good in a crisis as I have the ability not to scream which isn't to be confused with the tendency to shout. I shout but never scream. Your grandmother never screams but she indicates an emergency by pursing her lips.

Not screaming is a very good start to coping. As you have given no audible indication that there is an emergency, people will not be sure there is one and this gives you a small amount of breathing space. Breathe during this breathing space or you might forget later and faint, complicating matters. After that you require a clear head, a cool manner and decisive actions.

CRISES FROM OUR OWN LIVES
AND HOW I MANAGED

Crises can arise in many shapes and sizes and the
mother's job is to decide how big it is and avoid
escalation. A child might drop a glass when a father is
speaking on the phone, a mother's hair can catch fire, a
child can fall out of a tree, find herself in a house with
a burglar in it, or lose her keys again when her father
has just had a new set cut. She can fail an exam, have
a pet commit suicide, get dumped by the boy of her
dreams, or choke on a peach stone. All the above have
happened to us, as well as broken limbs and wounds
requiring many stitches. I will outline correct behaviour
in three instances which will give you the general drift.

THE DROPPED GLASS

Should the father be on the telephone to the bank and
a child drop a glass, smashing it within his earshot
and distracting him badly, the mother must first remove
the child from the scene, by the bicep if necessary, and
reassure her it is not a major problem despite the father
shaking his fist. The mother may then clear up the mess
quietly and without fuss or she may hand the father the
dustpan and brush and suggest he clear up the mess
himself while she takes the child to the park. This is
called diversion.

THE MOTHER'S HAIR ON FIRE

Should a mother's hair catch fire when she bends down to light the oven, she must not call out although she is in danger of imminent incineration. The children will already be calling out because they will want to know what has happened to the biscuits she was attempting to cook. The mother must grab a tea towel and beat out the flames, then she must cut off bits of singed hair and have a shower to remove all traces of burning smell which is frightening in the extreme. Then she should telephone her husband and hang up on him when he says, 'How one earth could you let a thing like that happen?' This is called direct action.

A BURGLAR IN THE HOUSE

In the event of a burglar breaking into a daughter's flat and the daughter phoning the mother to whisper in a voice full of fear and dread, 'Mumma, there's someone in the house,' and then to fall silent before screaming in a horrible and chill fashion, the mother should turn to the father and say, 'There is a burglar in her flat. Phone the police on the other line.' The mother should then call down the line, 'Are you there? Are you there? What's going on?' Then when it emerges that the burglar is an idiot boyfriend of her flat mate thinking he is being funny, the father should say, 'I'm getting down there to sort him out.' And then he should settle things amicably when it emerges the boyfriend is six foot four in every direction. This is called tactical retreat.

Rock

During such crises, you must not only be a rock, you must attend to the rest of family life and your own job without missing a beat. This can be very taxing and sometimes you will feel under siege. But the more it happens, the better you will be at it and the more you will realise there is nothing to it. It helps hugely to have a husband who will tackle large spiders and to have some sort of life beyond work and family which gives you light relief.

Keep beta-blockers in your drawer but don't take them.

Rule: Sometimes very loud shouting can be mistaken for screaming. This is not your fault. Shout if you must.

Hobbies, lovers
and so forth

In the early stages of your family life, you will have so few spare moments that the very idea of doing something on your own will strike you as laughable. But eventually, you will realise that unless you do something on your own, you will forget who you were, let alone are.

Does this matter? It does to the standard egomaniac, and to most wives and mothers eventually, because eventually they understand they have needs beyond the home (see Outgrowing earlier). Sooner or later, you need to rediscover your sense of self. There was nothing wrong with sublimating it when selflessness was a condition of the job but one day you need to get it back.

A JOB

This might be all you need. You might always have
gone out to work, found the job stimulating, the
people fascinating and made many interesting friends
who know you only for the charming, intelligent,
well-dressed person who never smells of old milk and
never loses her temper that they meet in the office.

The job on top of family life might be so exhausting
that you have absolutely nothing left in terms of time or
energy for anything else. But wait for it.

HOBBIES

After a while you will want to play tennis, play cards or
have a laugh with people who are not family and will
not expect you to talk family. You mightn't get to this
point for many years but when you do, recognise it and
feel no guilt. It's not an act of betrayal, only of survival.

LOVERS

Maybe you will be tempted to take a lover. This will
be for romance, adoration, excitement and distraction,
none of which will be on offer in the family home. It
may even be for sex. Perhaps your sex life has taken
a turn for the worse with children in the next room
listening. Is it worth it? All that deceit, all that trying
to find places to meet without being recognised and
then finding out that the lover isn't half the man your
husband is? Possibly. I wouldn't dream of advising you
but don't expect me to provide alibis for you because it
will place me awkwardly with my grandchildren. Should

you take a lover the rules I described earlier apply. It will be your burden. Shoulder it on your own.

YOUR HUSBAND

Whatever diversion you choose, lovers excepted, you need to make it completely plain to your husband that this isn't growing away, just recovering and that he is entitled to recover himself from the shock of losing himself. It might be that the hobbies you want to take up are hobbies you can take up together and that will be perfect.

I don't recommend wife-swapping, even though it's something you can do together, because it leads to all sorts of confusion. I don't know this for a fact because I have never done it but I can use my imagination. That is all you should do too. This is where all your accomplishments will come in. You will thank me for them one day.

Rule: Should you take up golf with your husband, do not wear matching clothes. That kind of togetherness is tragic.

MATURITY

Dear Daughters,

This is about as far as my guide can go because I have come to the point I have reached myself – old enough to have grown-up children but not old enough to be old. Ageing maybe, but you are ageing. Mature maybe, but you are maturing.

GETTING MATURE

The upside of being in my generation, the grandparents' generation, is that you know a lot more than you think, find fewer things important and take more things in your stride. You are better at your job and more confident in your opinions. All that is great.

The downside is you look like Camilla Parker Bowles who may be famous for her wit, intelligence and sexiness but is none the less painfully locked in a losing battle with time. She has looked like this for all of her public life. Maybe she has adopted an air of defeat to get people off her back. I don't know but I don't want it.

I am attempting to shake it off with haircuts, interesting use of bleach and non-surgical face-lifts. I am thinking about cosmetic dentistry, but only thinking. Maybe it will be too expensive and painful and I won't look any better after it has been done. I don't want my face to collapse as I understand can happen if they stick pole things in your jaw.

My shape has changed as yours will. It changed after I had my womb removed just after my fortieth birthday. After years of being a little angular, it grew infinitely more womanly. There's an irony. I didn't mind losing my womb since it had stood me in good stead producing three of the best children a mother could want.

Now is probably the time to stop thinking about my body and to expand my mind and spiritual life but bugger that. My mind expands and contracts all on its own depending on how much sleep I've had, how much I have drunk and whether or not I'm interested. As for my spiritual life, I'm still growing, still at the dabbling phase.

I have been married to your father for nine years longer than I was single which means that most of my growing I have done with him. In many ways, living with him has shaped me as much as living with my mother. I am now a woman who takes care to have the kitchen sort of tidy when he comes home from work because he hates it untidy and I can't bear him to walk straight in the door to pick up a dishcloth.

The same will happen to you. You will leave home and absorb the habits and outlook of your partner which means you will change from the children you are today. Probably you will look back on your upbringing and find some of it ridiculous. Well, it has been and you will learn from that just as you will have learnt from some of the other stuff that was sensible.

I don't know if this guide will be of any use. I don't suppose so. You are all very clever and sensible.

But I feel better for having written it. And I remain,
as always,

Your ever loving,
Mumma.